DEVELOPMENTAL PROFILES

Pre-Birth Through Eight

3rd Edition

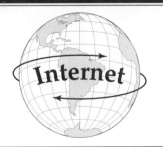

DEVELOPMENTAL PROFILES

Pre-Birth Through Eight

3rd Edition

K. Eileen Allen
Professor Emeritus,
University of Kansas

Lynn R. Marotz, Ph.D., R.N.
University of Kansas

Delmar Publishers

an International Thomson Publishing company I(T)P®

Albany • Bonn • Boston • Cincinnati • Detroit • London • Madrid
Melbourne • Mexico City • New York • Pacific Grove • Paris • San Francisco
Singapore • Tokyo • Toronto • Washington

Notice to the Reader

Publisher does not warrant or guarantee any of the products described herein or perform any independent analysis in connection with any of the product information contained herein. Publisher does not assume, and expressly disclaims, any obligation to obtain and include information other than that provided to it by the manufacturer.

The reader is expressly warned to consider and adopt all safety precautions that might be indicated by the activities herein and to avoid all potential hazards. By following the instructions contained herein, the reader willingly assumes all risks in connection with such instructions.

The publisher makes no representation or warranties of any kind, including but not limited to, the warranties of fitness for particular purpose or merchantability, nor are any such representations implied with respect to the material set forth herein, and the publisher takes no responsibility with respect to such material. The publisher shall not be liable for any special, consequential, or exemplary damages resulting, in whole or part, from the readers' use of, or reliance upon, this material.

Cover Design: Publisher's Studio

Delmar Staff
Publisher: William Brottmiller
Acquisitions Editor: Erin O'Connor Traylor
Production Coordinator: James Zayicek
Art and Design Coordinator: Jay Purcell
Editorial Assistant: Mara Berman

COPYRIGHT © 1999
by Delmar Publishers
an International Thomson Publishing company

The ITP logo is a trademark under license.
Printed in Canada

For more information, contact:

Delmar Publishers, Inc.
3 Columbia Circle, Box 15015
Albany, New York 12212-5015

International Thomson Editores
Seneca 53
Colonia Polanco
11560 Mexico D. F. Mexico

International Thomson Publishing Europe
Berkshire House
168-173 High Holborn
London, WC1V 7AA
United Kingdom

International Thomson Publishing GmbH
Königswinterer Straße 418
53227 Bonn
Germany

Nelson ITP, Australia
102 Dodds Street
South Melbourne,
Victoria, 3205 Australia

International Thomson Publishing Asia
60 Albert Street
#15-01 Albert Complex
Singapore 189969

Nelson Canada
1120 Birchmont Road
Scarborough, Ontario
M1K 5G4, Canada

International Thomson Publishing Japan
Hirakawa-cho Kyowa Building, 3F
2-2-1 Hirakawa-cho, Chiyoda-ku,
Tokyo 102, Japan

1 2 3 4 5 6 7 8 9 10 XXX 04 03 02 01 00 99 98

Library of Congress Cataloging-in-Publication Data

Allen, L. Eileen, 1918–
    Developmental profiles : pre-birth through eight / K. Eileen
Allen, Lynn R. Marotz. — 3rd ed.
        p..   cm.
    Includes bibliographical references and index.
    ISBN 0-8273-8605-2
    1. Child development.   I. Marotz, Lynn R.   II. Title.
RJ131.A496   1999
155.4—dc21   98-26634
                                               CIP

CONTENTS

PREFACE

Developmental Profiles opens with a brief overview of major issues in child development. This serves as a refresher of basic principles and background material for the several chapters on age-level expectancies that follow. The concluding chapters focus on when and where to seek help if there are concerns about a child.

Developmental Profiles is designed for:

- child development and early childhood students and teachers-in-training;
- child care providers in home care settings, child care centers, preschools, and Head Start programs, and nannies in the child's own home;
- allied health professionals from fields such as nursing, nutrition, audiology, social work, physical and occupational therapy, psychology, medicine, and language and speech therapy, as well as other disciplines providing services for young children and their families;
- parents, the most important contributors to a child's optimum development.

Developmental Profiles provides nontechnical information about:

- what to expect of young children at each succeeding stage of development;
- the ways in which all areas of development are intertwined and mutually supportive;
- the unique pathway that each child follows in a developmental process that is alike, yet different, among children of similar age;
- sequences, not age, being the critical concept in evaluating developmental progress;
- the use of developmental norms in teaching, observing, and assessing children and in designing individualized as well as group learning experiences.

Developmental Profiles includes a number of special features:

- A section that briefly defines and describes the most commonly encountered terms and concepts in the child development literature.
- Concise profiles of developmental domains at various age levels from prebirth through age eight.

- Developmental alerts for each level; that is, signals that indicate a possible delay or problem.
- Descriptions of daily activities and routines typical of children at each level.
- Where and how to get help if there is concern about a child's development.
- Web addresses for a number of professional organizations and information resources.
- A comprehensive developmental checklist to aid in the observation and screening process and a summary of early infant reflexes.
- An annotated bibliography for back-up and additional readings on child development, screening and assessment, referral and information resources.
- Color inserts highlighting child and family diversity and observing children in natural environments.
- A sample health history form and examples of frequently used screening and assessment instruments designed to evaluate infants, toddlers, and young children.

INTRODUCTION

The third edition of *Developmental Profiles: Prebirth to Eight* has been expanded and updated. At the same time, it maintains the authors' original intent: to provide a comprehensive yet nontechnical, easy-to-follow guide to early development. Major characteristics of each developmental domain for each age level continue to be in the original point-by-point format (Chapters 4 through 7). This arrangement has proven invaluable for teachers, students, parents and practitioners in readily accessing needed information. The Daily Routines for each age are easily located in the shaded boxes. The shading allows Routines to be quickly distinguished from Learning Activities and Developmental Alerts which are also noted. Glossary words, as in early editions, are in bold type throughout the text with each term defined at the bottom of the page on which it is used.

A number of special features and additions enhance the third edition. These include:

FULL-COLOR INSERTS ON DIVERSITY AND OBSERVATION OF CHILDREN

These new inserts have been included to draw the reader's attention to important contemporary issues. One insert focuses on diversity and the implications for teachers, caregivers, and allied practitioners. It showcases the range of cultural, economic, and developmental differences that characterize children and families in our schools and child care settings. Another insert addresses the all-important topic of observing children. Emphasis is placed on the value of systematic observation to ensure quality and individualized guidance in early childhood programs. Several observation strategies are described that teachers, parents, and students can use when observing children in naturalistic environments such as home and school.

SEVEN- AND EIGHT-YEAR-OLDS NOW DISCUSSED SEPARATELY

Though there is considerable overlap in development during these two years, sufficient differences exist to warrant the division now presented in Chapter 7. As always, the authors sound the warning that age level expectancies are based on averaging the behaviors and achievements of large numbers of children of similar age, in each area of development. Typically developing children, in real life, vary greatly from the norms.

CHAPTERS 8 AND 9

When to Seek Help (Chapter 8) has been updated, expanded, and the earlier list of screening instruments has been moved. More comprehensive and thoroughly updated lists are now located in Appendix 4. This all new appendix categorizes screening and assessment instruments separately. The instruments are grouped according to both general development and specific developmental areas. Where to Seek Help (Chapter 9) also has been rewritten to provide more resource information. Featured in this new edition are Web addresses for a number of professional organizations. These reputable sites contain a wealth of information on both general and specialized areas of interest.

ANNOTATED BIBLIOGRAPHY

The Annotated Bibliography is now located in Appendix 5. The references have been thoroughly updated while retaining those titles that have achieved classic status. Two new sections have been added: one on observing children, the other on diversity in a pluralistic society.

PHILOSOPHICAL NOTES

The common practice of dividing infancy and childhood into age-related units of months and years can distort the realities of human development. On the other hand, when describing developmental expectations, developmental progress, and delays, other systems seem to work even less well. Let it be stressed here, as it is again and again throughout the text, that the age specifications are only approximate markers derived from *averages* or *norms*. In a way, they can be thought of as midpoints not intended to represent any one child. Age expectations also can be thought of as summary terms for skills that vary from child to child in form and time of acquisition. The truly important consideration in assessing a child's development is *sequence*. The essential question is not chronological age but whether the child is moving forward step-by-step in each area of development. *Developmental Profiles* proves itself an invaluable resource in addressing this issue.

As in the first two editions of *Developmental Profiles*, the early days, weeks, and months of infancy are looked at in great detail. This is how it should be. Research findings on infant development are truly astonishing. What the newborn is capable of learning is indeed amazing. It is especially amazing in light of conventional wisdom implying that young babies simply flounder around in a kind of "booming, buzzing" confusion. Far from it! With more and more infants entering infant programs at ever earlier ages, it is most important that caregivers are knowledgeable about infant development and infant learning and that parents hold appropriate expectations and can describe to caregivers what they want and believe best for their infants.

The first year of life is critical in terms of foundation learnings in every area of development. The vast array of new and complex behaviors that toddlers and preschoolers must learn in three or four short years is also monumental. At no other period in a lifetime will so much be expected of an individual in so short a time. With other-than-parent child care being the norm rather than the exception, it is essential that caregivers and parents have a thorough knowledge of how young children grow and develop and learn. Thus, an underlying theme of *Developmental Profiles* continues to be partnership with parents. No matter how many hours a day the child is with caregivers, parents play the most significant role. They need to be encouraged to talk about their child, their observations, their concerns. These bits of information are integral to the well-being of each child. And always, when parents talk, professionals need to listen with focused attention and respond with genuine respect.

Partnership with parents becomes even more critical when an infant or child is suspected of having a developmental problem or irregularity. The Developmental Alerts following each age section can be especially useful to either a parent or teacher in initiating a discussion about their concerns. Let it be emphasized, however, that under no circumstances should this book or any other book be seen as an instrument for diagnosing a developmental problem. That is the job of clinicians.

The purposes of this text can be summed up as follows:

- to provide a concise review of developmental principles;
- to provide easily accessible information about what to expect at each developmental level;
- to suggest appropriate ways for adults to facilitate learning and development during the early years;
- to pinpoint warning signs of a possible developmental problem;
- to suggest how and where to get help;
- to emphasize the value of direct observation of children in all early childhood programs;
- to describe cultural and racial diversity in terms of its impact on the developmental process.

ACKNOWLEDGMENTS

The authors and Delmar Publishers thank the following reviewers for their valuable comments and suggestions.

Carolyn S. Cooper, Ph.D.
Eastern Illinois University
Charleston, IL

Margaret DiCarlo
New Hope Manor School
Kauneonga Lake, NY

Ruth R. Saxton, Ph.D.
Georgia State University
Atlanta, GA

Ann Schmidt
Champlain College
Burlington, VT

Wanda Smith
Petit Jean Technical College
Morrilton, AR

Gayle M. Stuber, Ph.D.
Baker University
Baldwin City, KS

Bette Talley, Ph.D.
Southeastern Bible College
Birmingham, AL

ABOUT THE AUTHORS

K. Eileen Allen taught at the University of Washington in Seattle and at the University of Kansas in Lawrence. When she retired after a total of thirty-one years of teaching at the two universities, she returned to Seattle. At both schools she taught child development, family relations, and early childhood education. She also trained teachers and supervised child development laboratory classrooms. Throughout her career she published textbooks and numerous research studies. Many of the publications focused on helping children with behavior and learning problems, others on an interdisciplinary approach to early intervention. Ten years into retirement finds her as busy as ever, revising her textbooks, reviewing articles submitted for publication, sitting on several boards, and doing a bit of consulting (Microsoft's early childhood ventures being a recent and exciting job). Advocating for children is still a priority. Currently her focus is on the Washington State Literacy Program and its efforts to introduce early literacy into low-income housing and child care projects.

Lynn R. Marotz is a faculty member of the Department of Human Development and Family Life, and also serves as the associate director of the Edna A. Hill Child Development Center at the University of Kansas. She brings her nursing background, training in education, and years of experience with children to the field of early childhood. Her primary interests include teacher training and administration, policy development, early identification of health impairments, and the promotion of wellness among young children. She teaches undergraduate and graduate courses in child development, administration, health, and nutrition. Her experience also includes extensive involvement with policy development, health screenings, working with parents and allied health professionals, and the referral process. She has made numerous professional presentations at state and national conferences, and has authored a variety of publications on children's health, identification of illness and developmental problems, environmental safety, and nutrition. In addition, she also serves on a number of state and local advisory boards.

CHAPTER 1

PRINCIPAL CONCEPTS IN CHILD DEVELOPMENT

The study of infant and child development has been a major focus of psychology since the 1920s. Throughout these years, there has been an ongoing disagreement known as the **heredity versus environment (nature/nurture) controversy.** Coming from both sides of the issue, a long line of researchers provide us with the principal concepts related to how children learn, how they grow, how they mature. Most of our current knowledge comes out of four major approaches: maturational, psychoanalytic, cognitive-developmental, and learning theory.

Maturational theory promotes a biological or *nature* approach to human development. Historically, Arnold Gessell is the significant figure in this area of developmental research. He assumed that development is governed mainly by internal forces that are of biologic and genetic origin.

Psychoanalytic theory implies that much of human behavior is governed by unconscious processes, some present at birth, others that develop over time. Sigmund Freud is the acknowledged originator of psychoanalytic theory as it applies to both child and adult development.

Cognitive-developmental theory is attributed to Jean Piaget, who theorized that children construct their own knowledge through active exploration of their environment. Four major stages of development emerge, two of which occur in the early years: first the sensorimotor stage, then the preoperational stage.

Learning theory, in its modern form, stems from the work of B. F. Skinner, who formulated a *nurture,* or environmental approach. He argued that development, for the most part, is a series of learned behaviors based on an individual's positive and negative interactions with his or her immediate world.

---

heredity versus environment (nature/nurture) controversy—Refers to whether development is primarily due to biological/genetic forces (heredity/nature) or to external forces (environment/nurture).

Current approaches to child development rarely rest on any one theory to the exclusion of the others. Each theory has made important contributions to our understanding of children. The majority of today's researchers dismiss the nature/nurture question as an improbable "either/or" proposition. They view development as an interaction of environmental influences and inborn characteristics.

To provide effective care and guidance for young children, it is essential that parents, caregivers, and teachers understand the principal concepts of child development that have emerged from the various theories. Each child's overall development and behavior can then be put in focus, day by day. Such understanding also gives a long-range perspective on each child. This two-track approach is indispensable in helping all children grow and develop in ways best suited to each as a unique individual.

The following key concepts have been selected because of their current importance and widespread use in the field of child development. As varied as these concepts are, it is necessary to understand and apply all of them in working effectively with infants and young children.

ESSENTIAL NEEDS

All children, those who are developing normally or typically, those who have developmental disabilities, and those who are **at-risk** for developing problems, have a number of physical and psychological needs in common. These needs must be met if infants and children are to survive, thrive, and develop to their best potential. Many developmental psychologists view the early years as the most critical in the entire life span. Never again will the child grow so rapidly or change so dramatically. During these very early years, children learn all of the many behaviors that characterize the human species—walking, talking, thinking, and socializing. Truly amazing, all of that within the first two or three years! And, never again will the child be so totally dependent on parents, caregivers, and teachers to satisfy the basic needs of life and to provide opportunities for learning.

To discuss essential needs in an orderly and logical fashion, they can be separated into groups. However, it must be understood that physical and psychological needs are interrelated and interdependent. Meeting a child's physical needs while neglecting psychological needs may lead to developmental problems. The opposite also is true—a child who is physically neglected frequently experiences trouble in learning and getting along with others.

---

at-risk—Term describing children who may be more likely to have developmental problems due to certain predisposing factors, such as premature birth, neglect, or inadequate nutrition.

Children need affection and positive
attention from adults.

Physical Needs

- Shelter and protection from harm.
- Food that is nutritious and appropriate to age of child.
- Warmth, adequate clothing.
- Preventive health and dental care; treatment of physical and mental conditions as needed.
- Cleanliness.
- Rest and activity, in balance.

Psychological Needs

- Affection and consistency—**nurturing** parents and caregivers who can be depended on to "be there" for the child.
- Security and trust—familiar surroundings with parents and caregivers who respond reliably to the needs of the infant and child.
- **Reciprocal** exchanges—beginning in earliest infancy "give-and-take" interactions that promote responsiveness in the child.
- Appropriate adult expectations as to what the child can and cannot do at each level of development.
- Acceptance and positive attitudes toward whatever cultural, ethnic, or developmental differences characterize the child.

---

nurturing—Nurturing includes qualities of warmth, loving, caring, and attention to physical needs.
reciprocal—Exchanges between individuals or groups that are mutually beneficial (or hindering).

Children need freedom to explore.

The Need to Learn

- Play is essential to early learning; infants and children need unlimited opportunities to engage in play in all of its many forms with freedom to explore and experiment, with necessary limits clearly stated and consistently maintained.
- Access to **developmentally appropriate** experiences and play materials.
- An appropriate "match" between a child's skill levels and the materials and experiences available to the child: enough newness to challenge, but not so much that the child feels incapable or excessively frustrated.
- Errors and failures treated as important steps in the learning process, never as reasons for condemning or ridiculing a child.
- Adults who demonstrate in everyday life the appropriate behaviors expected of the child, be it language, social interactions, or ways of handling stress. *Remember: parents and caregivers are major models of behavior for young children.* They also are a child's first teachers; children learn more from what adults do than from what they say.
- Inclusion in an active language "community," especially family and child care, in which the child learns to communicate through sounds, gestures, signs, and eventually words and sentences (either spoken, signed, or written).

---

developmentally appropriate practice (DAP)—Commonly used term that is now popularized in a handbook published by the National Association for the Education of Young Children (see bibliography).

**New skills are built on previously
learned skills.**

The Need for Respect and Self-Esteem

- A respectful and supportive environment in which the child's efforts are encouraged, approved, and supported: "You picked up your crayons. Good job! Shall I put them on the shelf for you?"
- Acceptance of the child's efforts; respect for accomplishments whether small or large, for errors as well as successes: "Look at that! You laced your shoes all by yourself." (No mention of the eyelet that was missed.)
- Recognition that accomplishment, the "I can do it" attitude, is the major and most essential component of a child's **self-esteem:** "You're really getting good at cutting out cookies!"
- Sincere attention to what the child is doing well; using **descriptive praise** to help children learn to recognize and respect their accomplishments: "You got your shoes on the right feet all by yourself!"
- Awareness of the tremendous amount of effort and concentration that goes into acquiring developmental skills; positive responses to each small step as a child works toward mastery of a complex skill such as self-feeding with a spoon. "Right! Just a little applesauce on the spoon so it stays on."

---

self-esteem—Feelings about one's self-worth.
descriptive praise—Words or actions that describe to a child specifically what she or he is doing correctly or well (as in the above example about shoes).

Learning through play.

NORMAL OR TYPICAL DEVELOPMENT

The terms *typical* and *normal*, when referring to the developing child, tend to be used interchangeably. They imply that a child is growing, changing, and acquiring a broad range of skills characteristic of the majority of children of similar age within the same culture. However, such a statement oversimplifies the concept. Additional factors must be considered. Normal or typical development also implies:

- An integrated process by which children change in orderly ways in terms of size, **neurological** structure, and behavioral complexity;
- A **cumulative** or "building block" process in which each new aspect of growth or development includes and builds on earlier changes; each accomplishment is necessary to the next stage or next set of skills;
- A continuous process of give and take (reciprocity) between the child and the environment, each changing the other in a variety of ways: The three-year-old drops a cup, breaks it, and the parent scolds the child. Both events, the broken cup and parent's displeasure, are environmental changes that the child triggered. From this experience the child may learn to hold on more firmly next time, and this constitutes a change in the child's behavior—fewer broken cups, thus less adult displeasure.

A number of other key concepts are closely related to the basic concept of normal development. These include:

---

neurological—Refers to the brain and nervous system.
cumulative—An add-on process, bit by bit or step by step.

Developmental Milestones

Developmental milestones are major markers or points of accomplishment in the development of motor, social, cognitive, and language skills. They show up in somewhat orderly steps and within fairly predictable age ranges. Milestone behaviors are those that most typically developing children are likely to display at approximately the same age. For example, almost every child begins to smile socially between four and ten weeks, and to speak a first word or two around twelve months. These achievements (social smile, first words) are but two of a number of significant behavioral indications that a child's developmental progress is on track. The failure of one or more developmental milestones to appear within a reasonable time frame indicates the need to observe the child carefully and systematically. (See the Developmental Alerts at the end of each age profile.)

Maturation

Maturation implies changes that are primarily biological: the appearance of new skills or behaviors common to human beings. Sitting, walking, and talking are examples of maturation. These skills do not come about independently of the environment however. Learning to walk, for example, involves muscle strength and coordination (influenced by adequate nutrition). Learning to walk also requires an environment that encourages practice, not only of walking as it emerges, but also of the behaviors and skills that preceded walking, such as rolling over, sitting, and crawling.

Sequences of Development

A sequence or pattern of development consists of predictable steps along a developmental pathway common to the majority of children. Children must be able to roll over before they can sit and sit before they can stand. *The critical consideration is the order in which children acquire these developmental skills, not their age in months and years.* The appropriate sequence in each area of development is an important indication that the child is moving steadily forward along a sound developmental **continuum.** In language development, for example, it does not matter how many words a child speaks by two years of age. What is important is that the child has progressed from cooing and babbling to "jabbering" (inflected **jargon**) to syllable production. The two- or three-year-old who has progressed through these stages usually produces words and sentences within a reasonable period of time.

---

continuum—A continuous pathway, an event following a preceding event.
jargon—Unintelligible speech; in young children, it usually includes sounds and inflections of the native language.

Sequence of motor development.

Developmental progress is rarely smooth and even. Irregularities, such as periods of **stammering** or the onset of a **food jag,** may characterize development. Regression, that is, taking a step or two backward now and again, is perfectly normal: a child who has been toilet trained may begin to have "accidents" when starting preschool or child care.

---

stammering—To speak in an interrupted or repetitive pattern.
food jag—A period when only certain foods are preferred or accepted.

Age-Level Expectancies or Norms

Age-level expectancies can be thought of as **chronological** or age-related levels of development. Investigators like Gesell and Piaget carried out systematic observations on infants and children of various ages. Analyses of their findings represent the average or typical age at which many specifically described developmental skills are acquired by most children in a given culture. This average age is often called the norm; thus a child's development may be described as at the norm, above the norm, or below the norm. For example, a child who walks at eight months is ahead of the norm (twelve to fifteen months), while a child who does not walk until twenty months is below the norm.

One point must be stressed: age-level expectancies *always represent a range and never an exact point in time* when specific skills will be achieved. Profiles of age expectancies for specific skills always should be interpreted as approximate midpoints on a range of months (as in the example on walking, from eight to twenty months with the midpoint at fourteen months). Once again, a reminder: it is *sequence* and *not age* that is the important factor in evaluating a child's progress.

Range of Typical or Normal Development

In real life, there is probably no child who is truly typical in every way. The range of skills and the age at which skills are acquired show great variation. This is true even among children who are described as being typical. Relevant again is the example of walking, one infant starting at eight months and another not until twenty months. Both are within the normal range, though many months apart on either side of the norm. No two children grow and develop at exactly the same rate, nor do they perform in exactly the same way. There are a half dozen perfectly normal ways of creeping and crawling. Most children, however, use what is referred to as contralateral locomotion, an opposite knee–hand method of getting about prior to walking. Also, some normally walking two-year olds never crawled, indicating great variation and a wide range of differences among children.

Organization and Reorganization

Development can be thought of as a series of phases. Spurts of rapid growth and development often are followed by periods of disorganization. Then the child seems to recover and move into a period of reorganization, "getting it all together" again. It is not uncommon for children to demonstrate behavior problems or even regression during these periods. The reasons vary. Perhaps the new baby has become an active and

---

chronological—Events or dates in sequence in the passage of time.

Behavior problems and regression are common.

engaging older infant who is now the center of family attention. Three-year-old brother may revert to babyish ways about the same time. He begins to have tantrums over minor frustrations and may, for the time being, lose his hard-won bladder control. Usually, these periods are short-lived. The three-year-old, for example, will almost always learn more age-appropriate ways of getting attention if given adequate adult support and understanding.

Interrelatedness of Developmental Areas

Discussions about development usually focus on several major areas: physical, motor, perceptual, cognitive, personal-social, and language. However, no single area develops independently of other developmental areas. Every skill, whether simple or complex, is a mixture. Social skills are an example. Why are some young children said to have good social skills? Often the answer is because they play well with other children and are sought out as playmates. To be a preferred playmate, a child must have many skills, all of them interrelated and interdependent. A four-year-old, for example, should be able to:

- Run, jump, climb, and build with blocks (good motor skills).

- Ask for, explain, and describe what is going on (good language skills).
- Recognize likenesses and differences among play materials and so select the right materials in a joint building project (good perceptual skills).
- Problem solve, conceptualize, and plan ahead in cooperative play ventures (good cognitive skills).

Every developmental area is well represented in the above example, even though social development was the primary area under consideration.

Individual Differences

A number of factors, in addition to genetic and biological, contribute to making each child unique, special, different from every other child.

Temperament. Temperament refers to an individual's responses to everyday happenings. Infants and young children differ in their activity level, alertness, irritability, soothability, restlessness, and cuddliness. Such qualities often lead to labels—the "easy" child, the "difficult" child, the "slow-to-warm" child. These characteristics (and labels) seem to have a definite effect on the ways that family, caregivers, and teachers respond to the child. This, in turn, reinforces the child's self-perceptions. For example, a slow-to-warm child may evoke few displays of affection from others and so perceive this as rejection which, in turn, makes it even more difficult for the child to act warm and outgoing.

Gender Roles. Early in life, young children learn the gender roles that are considered appropriate by their culture. Each boy and girl develops a set of behaviors, attitudes, and commitments that are defined, directly or indirectly, as acceptable male or female behaviors. In addition, each child plays out gender roles according to everyday experiences. In other words, each child's sense of maleness or femaleness will be influenced by playmates and play opportunities, toys, type and amount of television, and especially adult models (parents, neighbors, teachers).

Ecological Factors. Starting at conception, **ecology**—the environmental influence of family and home, community and society—affects all aspects of development. Listed below are ecological examples of powerful family and economic factors.

- Income level; adequacy of food and shelter.
- General health and nutrition of the pregnant woman; availability of pre- and postnatal care for mother and child.
- Parents' education level (number of the mother's years in school is a major predictor of a child's school achievement).

---

ecology—In terms of children's development, refers to interactive effects between children and their family, child care situation, school, and everything in the wider community that impacts their lives.

- Parents' understanding of obligations and responsibilities before and after the infant's birth.
- Patterns of communication and child rearing practices (loving or punishing, nurturing or neglectful); amount of family stress.
- Family structure—single- or two-parent, extended family, nontraditional household; foster homes.

Factors such as these contribute to each child being unlike any other child. For example, the child born to a single, fifteen-year-old parent living in poverty will be different from a child born and reared in a two-parent, working-class, or professional family.

Transactional Patterns of Development

From birth, the child begins to influence the behavior of parents and caregivers. In turn, parents and caregivers influence the child. Thus, development is a give-and-take process in which parents, caregivers, teachers, and the child are continuously interacting in ways that influence each other's behaviors. For example, a calm, cuddly baby expresses its needs in a clear and predictable fashion. This infant begins life with personal-social experiences that are quite different from those of a tense, colicky infant whose sleeping and eating patterns are highly irregular and, therefore, stressful to parents. The transactional process between infants and parents will be quite different in each instance and so will the developmental outcome.

Most infants and young children thrive when adults respond promptly and positively, at least a fair share of the time, to appropriate things a child says and does. Research indicates that children develop healthier self-concepts, as well as earlier and better language, cognitive, and social skills when raised by responsive adults.

ATYPICAL DEVELOPMENT

The term *atypical* is used to describe children with developmental differences, deviations, or marked delays: children whose development appears to be incomplete or inconsistent with typical patterns and sequences. The child with developmental delays performs in one or more areas of development like a much younger child. The child who is still babbling with no recognizable words beyond age three is an example of delayed development. This condition need not be disabling unless the child never develops **functional language.** Developmental deviation refers to an aspect of development that is different from what is ever seen in typical development. The child born with six

---

functional language—Language that allows children to get what they need or want.

toes or with a profound hearing loss has a developmental deviation. The six-toed child is not likely to be disabled while the child who is deaf may have a serious and, perhaps, lifelong disability. In any event, the concepts and principles described in the foregoing pages apply to the child with developmental differences as well as the child who is said to be developing typically. The principles outlined in this chapter provide the foundation for quality **inclusion programs** for all young children, regardless of their capabilities and backgrounds.

Test Your Knowledge

REVIEW QUESTIONS

1. List the four major developmental theories and give an identifying characteristic of each.

   a.

   b.

   c.

   d.

2. List three psychological needs of the developing child.

   a.

   b.

   c.

3. List three terms related to typical developmental progression.

   a.

   b.

   c.

---

inclusion programs—Community child care, school, and recreational facilities in which all children from the most gifted to the most disabled participate in the same activities. Inclusion is a federal law mandated by the Congress of the United States. Originally it was referred to as mainstreaming.

4. List three ways in which an adult can show respect for a young child's accomplishments.

    a.

    b.

    c.

5. List three ecological factors that influence early development.

    a.

    b.

    c.

TRUE OR FALSE

1. All that a child needs to develop fully is food, housing, clothing, and medical attention.

2. Errors, mistakes, and failures displayed by a young child provide opportunities for learning.

3. Each new accomplishment in a young child's development is built on earlier skills and experiences.

4. Environment has very little effect on a child's long-term development.

5. Maturation is biologically based (for the most part) and includes such things as learning to sit up, crawl, and walk.

6. The child with developmental delays is handicapped throughout life.

MULTIPLE CHOICE.   *Select one or more correct answers from the lists below.*

1. All areas of development are
    a. interrelated.
    b. interdependent.
    c. influenced by environment.

2. Development is
    a. cumulative, a building-block process.
    b. independent of neurological structure.
    c. physically and psychologically interactive.

3. Most normally developing children

   a. begin to smile between four and ten weeks.
   b. walk no later than one year.
   c. are talking in sentences by two years of age.

4. Development can be thought of as a series of phases that

   a. all children go through at the same age.
   b. show no regression; the child always goes forward, never backwards.
   c. are influenced by economic and cultural factors.

5. Children develop healthier self-concepts when adults provide

   a. contingent stimulation.
   b. frequent criticism and disapproval of errors the child makes.
   c. ample praise, especially descriptive praise.

CHAPTER 2

GROWTH AND DEVELOPMENT

BASIC PATTERNS AND CONCEPTS

When we look at a group of two-year-olds, five-year-olds, or eight-year-olds, we are struck by how similar they tend to be in size, shape, and abilities. At the same time, we note how different they are along these same dimensions. Both similarities and differences depend on a child's unique patterns of growth and development. What specifically

Growth is an increase in size.

do we mean by this complementary process, *growth and development?* Though the terms tend to be used interchangeably, they are not identical concepts.

Growth refers to specific physical changes and increases in the child's actual size. Additional numbers of cells, as well as enlargement of existing cells, account for the observable increases in a child's height, weight, head circumference, shoe size, length of arms and legs, and body shape. All growth changes lend themselves to direct and fairly reliable measurement.

The growth process is continuous throughout the life span. However, the rate of growth varies considerably according to age. For example, growth occurs rapidly during infancy and adolescence. In contrast, growth is slower and less dramatic in the preschool-age child. Throughout life, the body continues to repair and replace its cells.

Development refers to an increase in complexity, a change from relatively simple to more complicated and detailed. It involves an orderly progression along a continuous pathway on which the child acquires more refined knowledge, behaviors, and skills. The sequence is basically the same for all children. However, the rate of development may vary from child to child (see Chapter 1).

A child's rate and level of development are closely related to physiological maturity, especially of the nervous, muscular, and skeletal systems. Also, development is influenced by heredity and environmental factors unique to each individual. Together, these factors account for the wide range of variations in individual children's development.

Typical growth and development is a term used to indicate **acquisition** of certain skills and behaviors according to a predictable rate and sequence. As noted in Chapter 1, the range of what is considered normal is broad. It includes mild variations and simple irregularities: the three-year-old who lisps, the twelve-month-old who learns to walk without having crawled.

At-risk is a phrase used to describe infants and young children who have a high probability of developing physical problems, learning disabilities, or behavior difficulties. Examples might be: newborns who were premature and of low birth weight; infants whose mothers had poor nutrition during pregnancy; infants of very young parents. Early identification and intervention are of crucial importance with infants and children at-risk for developmental problems.

The term *atypical* is used to describe a child's growth or development that is incomplete or inconsistent with the normal sequence. Abnormal development in one area may or may not interfere with the development and mastery of skills in other areas. There are many reasons for atypical development including genetic errors, poor nutrition, illness, injury, and lack of opportunities to learn.

---

acquisition—The process of learning or achieving objectives (walking, counting, reading).

DEVELOPMENTAL AREAS

To describe and accurately assess children's progress, a developmental framework is needed. In this textbook we focus on six major developmental areas, or domains: physical; motor; perceptual; cognitive; speech and language; personal-social. Each area includes the many kinds of skills and behaviors that will be discussed in the developmental profiles (Units 4 through 7) that are the major focus of this book. Although these developmental areas, as noted earlier, are separated for the purpose of discussion, they cannot be separated from one another in reality. Each is integrally related to, and interdependent with, each of the others.

Developmental profiles or "word pictures" are useful for assessing both the immediate and ongoing status of children's skills and behavior. Keep in mind that the rate of development is uneven and occasionally unpredictable across areas, especially during the first two years of a child's life. For example, the language and social skills of infants and toddlers typically are less well developed than their ability to move about. Also, children's individual achievements may vary across developmental areas: a child may walk late, but talk early. Again, an important reminder: development in any of the areas is dependent on children having appropriate stimulation and adequately supported opportunities to learn.

Physical development and growth are the major tasks of early infancy and childhood. Understanding the patterns and sequences of physical development is essential to being effective parents, teachers, and caregivers. Healthy growth and development makes new learnings and behaviors possible, not adult pressure. A seven-month-old infant cannot be toilet trained; the **sphincter** muscles are not yet developed enough to exert such control. Nor can the majority of kindergartners catch or kick a ball skillfully—such coordination is impossible given a five- or six-year-old's stage of physical development—yet most of us have seen a Pee Wee League coach or parent reduce a child to tears for missing a catch or a kick.

Governed by heredity and greatly influenced by environmental conditions, physical development and growth is a highly individualized process. It is responsible for changes in body shape and proportions as well as overall body size. Growth, especially growth of the brain, occurs more rapidly during prenatal development and the first year than at any other time. Growth is intricately related to progress in other developmental areas. It is responsible for increasing muscle strength for movement, for depth perception in reaching for objects, and for improved muscular control for bladder training. The state of a child's physical development serves as a reliable index of general health and well-being. It also has a direct influence on determining whether children are likely to achieve their potential in each of the other developmental areas, including intellectual achievement.

---

sphincter—The muscles necessary to accomplish bowel and bladder control.

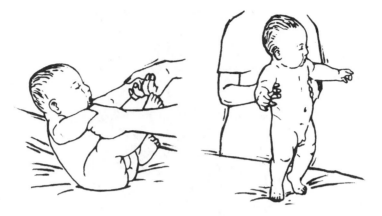

Cephalocaudal development proceeds from head to toe.

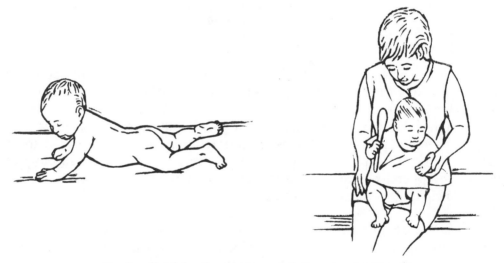

Proximodistal development proceeds from trunk outward.

Motor development refers to a child's ability to move about and control various body parts. Refinements in motor development depend on maturation of the brain, input from the sensory system, increased bulk and number of muscle fibers, a healthy nervous system, and opportunities to practice. This holistic approach to motor development contrasts markedly with the way early developmentalists saw the emergence of motor skills. They described a purely maturational process, instructions on children's genetic code. Today's psychologists consider such an explanation misleading and incomplete. Their research indicates that when young children show an interest, for example, in using a spoon to feed themselves, it is always accompanied by a hardening

**Motor refinement means the fine-tuning
of a skill.**

of wrist and finger bones, improved eye–hand coordination (to direct the spoon to the mouth), motivation (*liking* and *wanting* to eat what is in the bowl), and the drive to imitate what others are doing.

Motor abilities during very early infancy are purely **reflexive** and disappear as the child develops **voluntary** control. If these earliest reflexes do not phase out at appropriate times in the developmental sequence, it may be an indication of neurological problems (see Appendix 1). In such cases, medical evaluation should be sought.

Three principles govern motor development:

1. *Cephalocaudal:* bone hardening (ossification) and muscular development that proceeds from head to toe. The infant first learns to control muscles that support the head and neck, then the trunk, and later those that allow reaching. Muscles for walking develop last.
2. *Proximodistal:* bone hardening and muscular development that begins with improved control of muscles closest to the central portion of the body, gradually moving outward and away from the midpoint to the extremities (arms and legs). Control of the head and neck is achieved before the child can pick up an object with thumb and forefinger (pincer grasp or finger–thumb opposition).
3. *Refinement:* muscular development that progresses from the general to the spe-

---

reflexive—*Movements resulting from impulses of the nervous system that cannot be controlled by the individual.*
voluntary—*Movements that can be willed and purposively controlled and initiated by the individual.*

Habituation.

cific in both **gross motor** and **fine motor** activities. In the refinement of a gross
motor skill, for example, a two-year-old may attempt to throw a ball but
achieves little distance or control; the same child, within a few short years, may
pitch a ball over home plate with speed and accuracy. As for a fine motor skill,
compare the self-feeding efforts of a toddler with an eight-year-old who is moti-
vated (for whatever reason) to display good table manners!

Perceptual development refers to the increasingly complex use the child makes of information received through the senses: sight, hearing, touch, smell, taste, and body position. In one sense, perception is concerned with how any one or any combinations
of the senses are used. Perception also involves learning to select specific aspects of
the environment on which to focus. In other words, which details are important?
Which differences should be noted? Which should be ignored? These simple questions
demonstrate how difficult, if not impossible, it is to separate perceptual from cognitive
processes; thus our decision to combine perception and cognition.

Three aspects of perceptual development will be addressed:

---

*gross motor—Large muscle movements, such as locomotor skills (walking, skipping, swimming) and nonloco-
motive movements (sitting, pushing and pulling, squatting).*
*fine motor skills—Also referred to as **manipulative** skills; includes stacking blocks, buttoning and zipping,
and toothbrushing.*

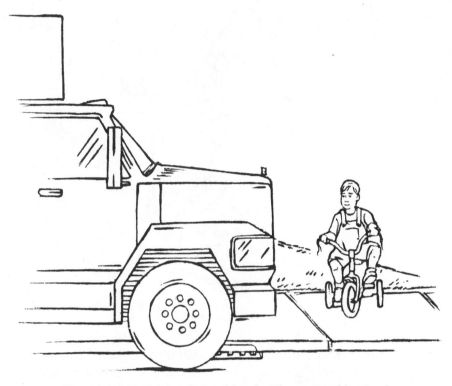

Sensory integration; seeing and hearing the approaching truck.

1. *Multimodality:* Information is generally received through more than one sense organ at a time; when listening to a speaker, we use sight (watching facial expressions and gestures) and sound (listening to the words).
2. *Habituation:* This is the ability to ignore everything except what is most important to the immediate situation; the child who is unaware of a telephone conversation in the background and focuses, instead, on her book.
3. *Sensory integration:* The child translates **sensory information** into functional behavior; the five-year-old sees a truck coming and waits on the curb for it to pass.

Rudiments of the perceptual system are in place at birth. Through experience, learning, and maturation it develops into a smoothly coordinated operation for processing complex information (sorting shapes according to size and color) and making fine discriminations (hearing the difference among initial sounds in rhyming words, such as rake, cake, lake). The sensory system also enables the individual to respond

---

sensory information—*Information received through the senses: eyes, ears, nose, mouth, touch.*

appropriately to all kinds of messages and signals: smiling in response to a smile; keeping quiet in response to a frown.

Cognitive development has to do with the expansion of a child's intellect or mental abilities. Cognition involves recognizing, processing, and organizing information and then using the information appropriately. The cognitive process includes such mental activities as discovering, interpreting, sorting, classifying, and remembering information. In older children it means evaluating ideas, making judgments, solving problems, understanding rules and concepts, thinking ahead, and visualizing possibilities or consequences. Cognitive development is an ongoing process of interaction between the child and objects or events in the environment.

Cognitive development begins with the reflexive behaviors that permit survival and primitive learning in the newborn. Next comes what Piaget has labeled the stage of sensorimotor activity. This stage lasts until approximately age two. The sensorimotor period is followed by a time of preoperational activity (another Piagetian term) that allows young children to internally process information coming in through their senses. Again it must be stressed that it is difficult, if not impossible, to discuss cognition as a separate developmental area, especially in the earliest years. Always there is overlap with both perceptual development and motor involvement. As the child matures, a further complication comes about—the overlap with language development.

Language Development. Language is often defined as a system of symbols, spoken, written and gestural (waving, scowling, cowering). It is a system that allows humans to communicate with one another. Normal language development is regular and sequential. It depends on maturation as well as learning opportunities. The first year of life is called the prelinguistic or prelanguage phase. This is a period when the child is totally dependent on body movements and nonword sounds such as crying and laughing to convey needs and feelings. This is followed by the linguistic or language stage, in which speech becomes the major way of communicating. Words and grammatical rules are acquired as children gain skill in conveying their thoughts and ideas through language.

Most children seem to understand a variety of concepts and relationships long before they have the words to describe them. In other words, the child has acquired receptive language, a skill that precedes expressive language (the ability to use words to describe and explain). Speech and language development is related to the child's general cognitive, social, perceptual, and neuromuscular development. Language development also depends on the type of language the child hears in the family and in the community.

Personal and social development is a broad area that concerns how children feel about themselves and their relationships with others. It refers to children's behaviors and responses to play and work activities, attachments to parents and caregivers, and relationships with brothers, sisters, and friends. Gender roles, independence, morality, trust, accepting rules and laws—these, too, are basic aspects of personal and social development. The family and its cultural values are also influential factors in shaping a child's social development and determining much of a child's basic personality.

In describing personal and social development, it must be remembered once again that children develop at different rates. Individual differences in genetic endowment, cultural background, health status, and a host of other environmental factors, such as experiences in child care, contribute to these variations. Therefore, no two children can ever be exactly alike, not in social development or in any other area of development.

AGE DIVISIONS

The age divisions throughout this book are commonly used by many child developmentmentalists when describing significant changes within developmental areas:

Infant	birth to one month
	1–4 months
	4–8 months
	8–12 months
Toddler	12–24 months
	24–36 months
Preschool	3–5 years
Primary School	6–8 years

Age divisions are to be used with extreme caution and great flexibility when dealing with real children. They are based on the averaged achievements, abilities, and behaviors of many children at various stages in development. As stated again and again, there is great variation from one child to another. It is the *appropriate* sequential acquisition of developmental tasks, *not age,* that is the major index to healthy development.

Test Your Knowledge

REVIEW QUESTIONS

1. List three factors that influence a child's rate of development.

   a.

   b.

   c.

2. List three factors that may lead to atypical development.

   a.

   b.

   c.

3. List three sources of perceptual information.

   a.

   b.

   c.

TRUE OR FALSE

1. The terms *growth* and *development* are interchangeable.

2. The rate at which a child develops is identical to all other children of the same age and gender.

3. Premature infants are often at-risk for developmental problems.

4. Adequate nutrition during the mother's pregnancy can have a beneficial effect on the child's development after it is born.

5. Growth of the brain occurs most rapidly during the latter part of the prenatal period and the first year of life.

6. Perceptual development depends on firsthand experiences: what the infant sees, hears, smells, tastes, and touches.

7. The perceptual system is in place at birth.

8. Receptive language develops after expressive language.

MULTIPLE CHOICE   *Select one or more correct answers from the lists below.*

1. Development is

   a. a change from simple to complex skills.

   b. a sequential process that is basically the same for all children.

   c. variable in terms of rate—that is, some children may walk earlier than others but talk later and still be considered normal.

2. Motor development during early infancy

   a. is almost entirely reflexive.

   b. is entirely voluntary.

   c. can be speeded up with direct teaching and intensive practice sessions.

3. Which of the following terms are associated predominantly with motor development?

   a. sensory integration

   b. proximodistal

   c. cephalocaudal

4. Which of the following terms apply to perceptual development?

   a. sensory integration

   b. racial integration

   c. school integration

5. Personal and social development are influenced by

   a. heredity.

   b. general health.

   c. culture.

6. Growth is

   a. measurable.

   b. faster during the preschool years than during infancy.

   c. continuous, in one form or another, throughout most of life.

CHAPTER 3

PRENATAL DEVELOPMENT

Each of the approximately 266 days of prenatal development (from **conception** to birth) is critical to producing a healthy newborn. **Genes** inherited from the baby's mother and father determine certain physical characteristics and, perhaps, temperament traits. However, because it is the mother who provides everything physically essential (as well as harmful) to the growing fetus, she plays a major role in promoting its healthy development. Her own health and nutritional status, both before and during pregnancy, strongly influence the birth of a healthy baby. When the father provides caring support for the mother throughout the pregnancy their unborn infant's development may be enhanced. Therefore, it is important that patterns of normal prenatal development, as well as practices that both facilitate and interfere with this process, are clearly understood by every potential parent.

THE DEVELOPMENT PROCESS

The prenatal period is commonly divided into stages. In obstetrical practice, pregnancy is classified according to trimesters, each consisting of three calendar months:

- first trimester—conception through the third month
- second trimester—fourth through the sixth month
- third trimester—seventh through the ninth month

---

conception—*The joining of a single egg or ovum from the female and a single sperm from the male.*
genes—*Genetic material that carries codes, or information, for all inherited characteristics.*

Pregnancy also may be discussed in terms of fetal development. This approach emphasizes critical changes that occur week by week and also encompasses three stages:

- germinal
- embryonic
- fetal

The *germinal stage* refers to the first fourteen days of pregnancy. The union of an ovum and sperm produces a zygote. Soon afterward, cell division begins, gradually forming a pinhead-size mass of specialized cells called a blastocyst. Around the fourteenth day, this small mass attaches itself to the wall of the mother's uterus. Successful attachment (**implantation**) marks the beginning of the **embryo** and the embryonic stage.

The *embryonic stage* includes the third through eighth weeks of a pregnancy. This stage is critical to the overall development of the fetus. Continuing cell divisions result in specialized cell layers that gradually form major organs and systems, such as the heart, lungs, and brain. Many of these structures will be functional near the end of this period. Embryonic blood, for example, begins to flow through the fetus's primitive cardiovascular system (heart and blood vessels) in the fourth to the fifth week.

During this time, other important changes are taking place. Once implantation is completed, a placenta begins to form. It serves four major purposes:

- to supply nutrients and hormones to the fetus
- to remove fetal waste products throughout the pregnancy
- to filter out many harmful substances, as well as viruses and other disease-causing organisms. (Unfortunately, many drugs can get through the placenta's filtering system.)
- to act as a temporary immune system by supplying the fetus with the same antibodies the mother produces against certain infectious diseases. (In most instances, the infant is protected for approximately six months following birth.)

An umbilical cord, containing two arteries and one vein, develops as the placenta is forming. This cord establishes a linkage between the fetus and the mother, affected by her health and general lifestyle. At this point, the fetus is highly vulnerable to any chemical substances and infectious illnesses that enter the mother's body. Exposure to these substances can seriously damage a fetus's major organs and systems that are developing at this time. As we will see in a later section, the result may be irreversible birth defects, ranging from mild to severe.

---

implantation—The attachment of the blastocyst to the wall of the mother's uterus; occurs around the twelfth day.
embryo—The cell mass from the time of implantation through the eighth week of pregnancy.

The *fetal stage* refers to the ninth week of pregnancy until birth (generally the thirty-eighth week). Most systems and structures are now formed and so, this final and longest period is devoted to growth and maturity. By the twelfth week, eyelids, lips, fingers, and toes are present and gender can be determined. Around the sixteenth week, the mother begins to feel the fetus moving. By the twenty-eighth week, the respiratory, circulatory, and nervous systems are sufficiently developed so that the infant can survive if born prematurely. During the final two months, few developmental changes occur. Instead, there are rapid and important gains in weight and size; a seven-month-old fetus weighs 2 to 3 pounds (0.9–1.4 kg) and will gain approximately 1/2 pound (0.23 kg) per week until birth. Body systems also are maturing and growing stronger, improving the fetus's chances of surviving outside the mother's body.

PROMOTING OPTIMUM FETAL DEVELOPMENT

Critical aspects of development are taking place during the earliest days of pregnancy, often before pregnancy has even been confirmed. Therefore, it is important that both mother and father practice healthy lifestyles throughout their reproductive years. Current research provides essential information about many factors that can improve a mother's chances of having a healthy baby, including:

- professional prenatal care
- good nutrition
- sufficient rest
- moderate weight gain
- regular exercise
- positive emotional state
- mother's age and general health

Prenatal Care

Medically supervised prenatal care is critical for ensuring the development of a healthy baby. Arrangements for such care should be made as soon as a woman suspects that she is pregnant. During the initial visit to a health care provider, pregnancy can be confirmed (or refuted), and any medical problems the mother might have can be evaluated and treated. Counseling on practices that influence fetal development will also be provided. For example, mothers may be encouraged to participate in a program of regular noncontact exercise. (As long as there are no complications, regular exercise can improve weight control, circulation, muscle tone, and elimination, and is believed to contribute to an easier labor and delivery.)

**Good nutrition is essential
during pregnancy.**

Nutrition

A mother's nutritional status, determined by what she eats before and during pregnancy, has a significant effect on her own health, as well as on that of the developing fetus. Good maternal nutrition lessens the risk of having a low birth weight or premature baby, two conditions often associated with serious developmental problems. Pregnancy increases a woman's dietary need for calories (energy), proteins, fluids, and certain vitamins and minerals, such as folacin, vitamins C and D, iron, and calcium. While vitamin supplements are generally prescribed, they must not be considered a substitute for a nutritious diet. Essential nutrients and calories must be supplied before the body can fully utilize vitamins in tablet form.

Weight

What is the optimum weight gain during pregnancy? This question has been debated for decades. Today, most medical practitioners agree that a woman should gain between 25 and 30 pounds (10–11.4 kg) over the nine-month period. Gains considerably under or over this range can increase risks for both mother and child during pregnancy and at birth. Following a diet that is nutritionally adequate helps ensure optimum weight gain. Consuming too many "empty" calories, such as those in junk foods, sweets, and alcohol, often leads to excessive weight gain. It also deprives both mother and fetus of critical nutrients found in a well-balanced diet.

Rest and Stress

Pregnancy often increases fatigue and strain on the mother's body. Additional sleep and occasional periods of rest may help ease these problems. Pregnancy also may induce or increase emotional stress. Prolonged or excessive stress can have negative effects on the fetus by reducing breathing rate, heart beat, and activity level. While it may not be possible for a pregnant woman to avoid all stress, strain, and fatigue, the ill effects can be lessened with proper rest, nutrition, and exercise.

Age and General Health

A woman's age at the time of conception is an important factor in fetal development. Numerous studies conclude that the early twenties to early thirties are the optimum years for childbearing. The rate of death and developmental disability among babies born to teenage mothers is nearly double that of babies born to women in their twenties. The immaturity of a teenager's reproductive system also increases the risk of giving birth to premature or low birth weight babies. In addition, teen mothers often lack access to prenatal care, adequate nourishment, and housing, and also have limited education, especially about caring for a child.

Pregnancy in older women (late thirties and beyond) presents other concerns. Genetic material contained in the ova gradually deteriorates as a woman ages, thus increasing the probability of certain birth defects, such as Down syndrome. New studies also suggest the quality of a male's sperm may lessen with age and exposure to environmental hazards, thus increasing the risk of damaged chromosomes that can cause birth defects. Older women also tend to experience a higher incidence of medical problems during pregnancy. However, greater awareness of good nutrition, exercise, and medical supervision can improve a mother's chances of having a healthy baby.

Increased knowledge and sophisticated technology are also contributing to reduction in fetal risk for mothers of all ages. Better genetic counseling, ultrasound scanning (**sonogram**), **CVS, amniocentesis,** and new blood tests allow medical personnel to

---

sonogram—Visual image of the developing fetus created by directing high-frequency soundwaves (ultrasound) at the mother's uterus; used to determine fetal age and physical abnormalities.
CVS—Chorionic Villus Sampling; a genetic screening procedure in which a needle is inserted and cells removed from the outer layer of the placenta; performed between the eighth and twelfth weeks to detect some genetic disorders, such as Down syndrome.
amniocentesis—Genetic screening procedure in which a needle is inserted through the mother's abdomen into the sac of fluids surrounding the fetus to detect some abnormalities, such as Down syndrome or spina bifida; usually performed between the twelfth and sixteenth weeks.

closely monitor fetal growth and detect specific problems early. These procedures are especially useful for many of today's women who are electing to delay childbearing until their late thirties and early forties.

While the risks of pregnancy are undeniably greater for older women and teen-agers, the problems often have as much to do with lack of knowledge and poverty as with age. (Exceptions are the chromosomal abnormalities such as Down syndrome.) Vast numbers of fetal problems, regardless of maternal age, are closely associated with lack of medical care, poor nutrition, substandard housing, and limited education, all closely associated with poverty.

THREATS TO OPTIMUM FETAL DEVELOPMENT

While much is known about how to have a healthy baby, there is also much known about the substances and maternal practices that lower those odds. Factors that have negative effects on the developing fetus are known as **teratogens.** Some are especially damaging during the earliest weeks of pregnancy. It is during these sensitive or critical periods that various fetal structures and major organ systems are rapidly forming and, thus, are most vulnerable to the effects of any harmful substance. The length of these critical periods varies: for example, heart—third to the sixth week, palate—sixth to the eighth week. Teratogens that have been identified through extensive research include:

- consumption of alcohol
- maternal smoking
- addictive drugs (e.g., cocaine, heroin, amphetamines)
- hazardous chemicals (e.g., mercury, lead, carbon monoxide, PCBs); radiation
- some medications, among them tranquilizers, hormones, antihistamines
- maternal infections (e.g., rubella [German measles], syphilis, herpes, cyto-megalovirus, AIDS, toxoplasmosis).

Researchers also are examining several controversial issues to determine whether there is any possible link to birth defects. Some of these include:

- prolonged exposure to high temperatures (hot baths, saunas, hot tubs)
- pesticides and insecticides
- secondary smoke
- certain over-the-counter medications
- electromagnetic fields, such as those created by heating pads and electric blankets
- caffeine

---

teratogens—Harmful agents that can cause fetal damage during the prenatal period.

Because many substances can, and do, cross the placental barrier, women who are even contemplating pregnancy should avoid unnecessary contact with known teratogens. As noted earlier, fetal organs and body systems are especially vulnerable to such agents during the first weeks following conception. This is not to imply that there is ever a completely "safe" period. Even in the later months, fetal growth can be seriously affected by maternal exposure to, or use of, substances mentioned here and in the following sections.

Alcohol

A mother's alcohol consumption during pregnancy can have serious consequences for the developing fetus. It can result in what now is diagnosed as fetal alcohol syndrome (FAS) or fetal alcohol effect (FAE). Children with FAS display a variety of abnormalities, including stunted growth, mental retardation, facial irregularities, heart defects, and behavior and learning problems. The incidence of fetal death is also greater. How much alcohol it takes to damage the fetus has not been determined; as little as an ounce or less per day (an amount once considered "safe") may affect the unborn baby. Thus, it is probably wise to limit the use of alcohol during the childbearing years, and to avoid it completely during pregnancy.

Smoking

Fetal malformations and birth complications have been linked to maternal smoking. Cigarette smoke contains substances, such as nicotine and carbon monoxide, which cross the placental barrier and interfere with normal fetal development. Carbon monoxide, for example, reduces the amount of oxygen available to the fetus; this early oxygen deprivation seems to correlate with learning and behavior problems, especially as exposed children reach school age. Also, babies of mothers who smoke tend to be of below-average birth weight; they are also more likely to be miscarried, premature, stillborn, or die shortly after birth.

Chemicals and Drugs

Numerous chemicals and drugs are also known to have an adverse effect on the developing fetus; these substances range from prescription medications to pesticides and "street" drugs. Some cause severe malformations, such as missing or malformed limbs or facial features. Others lead to fetal death (spontaneous abortion), premature birth, or behavior and learning disabilities during childhood and youth. Not all exposed fetuses will be affected in the same manner or to the same degree. The nature and severity of an infant's abnormalities seem to be influenced by the timing of exposure during fetal development, as well as the amount and type of substance. Research does not yet provide a definitive answer as to which drugs and chemicals (if any) have absolutely no harmful effects on the developing fetus; therefore, women who are or may become pregnant should be extremely cautious about using any chemical substance or medication except under medical supervision. They should also avoid exposure to previously discussed environmental hazards, particularly in the early stages of pregnancy.

Maternal Infections

While the placenta effectively filters out many infectious organisms, it cannot prevent all disease-causing agents from reaching the unborn child. Some of these agents are known to cause fetal abnormalities. The type of abnormality depends on the mother's illness and stage of pregnancy when infection occurs. For example, a pregnant woman who develops rubella (German measles) during the first four to eight weeks following conception is at high risk for giving birth to an infant who has heart problems, or is deaf, blind, or both (an example of the extreme vulnerability of the fetus during its earliest weeks).

Note: Rubella can be controlled if women who do not have natural immunity receive vaccinations after or not less than three to four months prior to pregnancy.

Fortunately, only a small percentage of babies exposed to infectious agents will experience abnormalities. It is still unknown why only some babies are affected. What is reasonably certain is that pregnant women who are well nourished, have good prenatal care, and are generally healthy and free of addictive substances and other excesses have a high probability of giving birth to a strong and healthy baby.

$$\boxed{\textit{Test Your Knowledge}}$$

REVIEW QUESTIONS

1. Identify three practices that improve a mother's chances of having a healthy baby:

   a.

   b.

   c.

2. List three factors that appear to be hazardous to fetal development:

   a.

   b.

   c.

3. Identify one characteristic of fetal development that occurs during each stage:

    a.

    b.

    c.

TRUE OR FALSE

1. A father's health status has no effect on the unborn child.
2. The younger a mother, the healthier her baby will be.
3. The embryonic stage is the most critical in terms of fetal development.
4. A zygote results when an egg and sperm unite.
5. Pregnancy increases a mother's need for calcium, iron, folacin, and vitamins C and D.
6. The placenta is effective in protecting a fetus from all harmful substances.
7. Maternal smoking can cause lowered birth weight.
8. Pregnant women should avoid exercise because it can cause a miscarriage.

MULTIPLE CHOICE *Select one or more correct answers from the lists below:*

1. Women over age thirty-five
   a. often have more difficulty getting pregnant.
   b. make better mothers because they are more mature.
   c. run a greater risk of having a child with a developmental defect.
2. Teratogens are
   a. more harmful to the fetus in the early weeks of pregnancy.
   b. substances that interfere with normal fetal development.
   c. the products of early cell division.
3. During pregnancy, poverty typically increases the risks to mother and fetus because
   a. prenatal care often is not available.
   b. a nutritionally adequate diet may be lacking.
   c. substance abuse is common.

4. Fetal abnormalities can be detected early in the pregnancy by

    a. amniocentesis.

    b. x-ray.

    c. sonograms.

5. Mothers who smoke during pregnancy are more likely to give birth to babies who

    a. have allergies.

    b. are born prematurely and have below-average birth weight.

    c. experience behavior and learning problems.

THE INFANT

NEWBORN (BIRTH TO ONE MONTH)

The healthy newborn infant is truly amazing. Within moments of birth it begins to adapt to an outside world that is radically different from the one experienced **in utero.** All body systems are in place and ready to function at birth. The newborn's body immediately assumes responsibility for breathing, eating, elimination, and regulation of body temperature. However, these systems are still immature; the newborn is completely dependent on parents and caregivers for survival.

Motor development (movement) is both reflexive and protective. There is no voluntary control of the body during the early weeks. Although newborn babies sleep most of the time, they do not lack awareness. They are sensitive to their environment and have unique methods of responding to it. Crying is their primary method of communicating needs and emotions. Perceptual and cognitive abilities are present, but they are primitive and impossible to distinguish from one another.

DEVELOPMENTAL PROFILES AND GROWTH PATTERNS

Growth and Physical Characteristics

The newborn's physical characteristics are unique from those of a slightly older infant. The skin is wrinkled. Within the first few days it will dry out and possibly peel in some areas. Skin color of all babies is relatively light, but will gradually darken to a shade characteristic of their genetic background. The head may appear to have an unusual shape as the result of the birth process, but it will assume a normal shape within the first week. Hair color and amount vary.

---

in utero—*The period when a fetus is developing in the mother's uterus.*

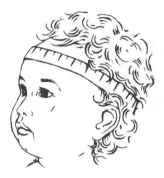

Head circumference.

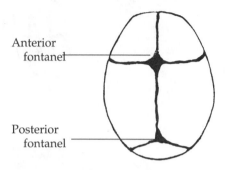

Anterior fontanel

Posterior fontanel

Fontanels.

- Average weight at birth is 6.5 to 9 pounds (3.0–4.1 kg); females weigh approximately 7 pounds (3.2 kg), males 7.5 pounds (3.4 kg).
- 5 to 7 percent of birth weight is lost in the days immediately following birth.
- Average gains of 5 to 6 ounces (0.14–0.17 kg) per week during the first month.
- Average length at birth ranges from 18 to 21 inches (45.7–53.3 cm).
- Respiration rate is approximately thirty to fifty breaths per minute; breathing may be somewhat irregular in rhythm and rate.
- Chest appears small and cylindrical; it is nearly the same size as the head.
- Normal body temperature ranges from 96°F to 99°F (35.6–37.2°C).
- Regulation of body temperature is irregular during the first few weeks due to immature body systems and a thin fat layer beneath the skin.
- Skin is sensitive, especially on the hands and mouth.
- Head is large in relation to body; accounts for nearly one-fourth of the total body length.
- Head circumference averages 12.5 to 14.5 inches (31.7–36.8 cm) at birth.
- "Soft" spots (**fontanels**) are located on the top (anterior) and back (posterior) of the head.
- Tongue appears large in proportion to mouth.
- Cries without tears.
- Eyes are extremely sensitive to light.
- Sees outlines and shapes; unable to focus on distant objects.

Motor Development

The newborn's motor skills are purely reflexive movements and are designed primarily for protection and survival. During the first month, the infant gains some control

---

fontanels—Small openings (sometimes called "soft spots") in the infant's skull bones, covered with soft tissue. Eventually they grow closed.

over several of these early reflexes. Gradually, many of these reflexes disappear as the infant's central nervous system matures and begins to take over control of purposeful behavior. During the first month the infant

- Engages in motor activity that is primarily reflexive:
  —Swallowing, sucking, gagging, coughing, yawning, blinking, and elimination reflexes are present at birth.
  —Rooting reflex is triggered by gently touching the sensitive skin around the cheek and mouth; the infant turns toward the cheek being stroked.
  —Moro (startle) reflex is set off by a sudden loud noise or touch, bumping of the crib, or quick lowering of the infant's position downward (as if dropping); both arms are thrown open and away from the body, then quickly brought back together over the chest.
  —Grasping reflex occurs when the infant tightly curls its fingers around an object placed in its hand.
  —Stepping reflex involves the infant moving the feet up and down in walking-like movements when held upright with feet touching a firm surface.
  —Tonic neck reflex (TNR) occurs when the infant, in supine (face up) position, extends arm and leg on the side toward which the head is turned; the opposite arm and leg are flexed (pulled in toward the body); this is sometimes called the "fencing position."
  —Plantar reflex is the curling of toes when pressure is placed against the ball of the foot.

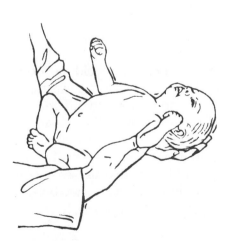

Moro relfex.

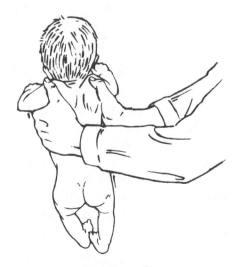

Stepping reflex.

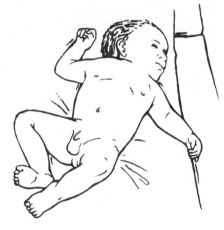

Tonic neck reflex (TNR).

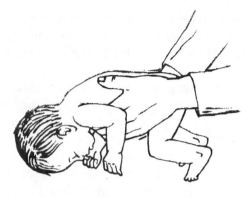

Prone suspension.

- Maintains "fetal" position (back flexed or rounded, extremities held close to the body, knees drawn up), especially when asleep.
- Holds hands in a fist; does not reach for objects.
- When held in a prone (face down) position, baby's head falls lower than the horizontal line of the body with hips flexed and arms and legs hanging down.
- Has good muscle tone in the upper body when supported under the arms.
- Turns head from side to side when placed in a prone position.
- **Pupils** dilate (enlarge) and constrict (become smaller) in response to light.
- Eyes do not always work together and may appear crossed at times.
- Attempts to track (follow) objects that are out of direct line of vision; unable to coordinate eye and hand movements.

Perceptual-Cognitive Development

The newborn's perceptual-cognitive skills are designed to capture and hold the attention of parents and caregivers and to gain some sense of the environment. Hearing is the most well developed of the skills. Newborns can hear and respond to differences among certain sounds and are especially responsive to mother's voice. Sounds and movements, such as cooing, rocking, and jiggling seem to be soothing. Newborns also are responsive to touch, with skin around the mouth and hands being especially sensitive. Vision is present, although limited. The newborn can focus both eyes, see objects up close, and follow slowly moving objects. From the earliest days of life, newborns absorb information through all of their senses, learning from what they see, hear,

pupils—The small, dark, central portion of the eye.

Studies own hand.

touch, taste, and smell. The newborn's cognitive behaviors can, thus, be characterized as purely reflexive. These take the form of sucking, startle responses, grimacing, flailing of arms and legs, and uncontrolled eye movements, all of which overlap with perceptual responses. During the first month the infant

- Blinks eyes in response to fast-approaching object.
- Follows a slowly moving object through a complete 180-degree arc.
- Follows objects moved vertically if object is close to infant's face (10–15 inches [25.4–38.1 cm]).
- Continues looking about, even in the dark.
- Begins to study own hand when lying in TNR position.
- Hearing is present at birth, and is more acute than vision. Infants hear as well as adults, except for quiet sounds.
- Prefers to listen to mother's voice rather than a stranger's.
- Often synchronizes body movements to speech patterns of parent or caregiver.
- Distinguishes some tastes; shows preference for sweet liquids.
- Sense of smell present at birth; will turn away from strong, unpleasant odors.

Speech and Language

The beginnings of speech and language development can be identified in several of the newborn's reflexes. These include the bite-release action that occurs when the infant's gums are rubbed, the rooting reflex, and the sucking reflex. In addition, the new baby communicates directly and indirectly in a number of other ways.

- Crying and fussing are major forms of communication at this stage.
- Reacting to loud noises by blinking, moving, stopping a movement, shifting eyes about, or making a startle response.
- Showing a preference for certain sounds, such as music and human voices, by calming down or quieting.

- Turning head in response to voice on either side.
- Making occasional sounds other than crying.

Personal-Social Development

Newborns possess a variety of built-in social skills. They indicate needs and distress and respond to parent's or caregiver's reactions. The infant thrives on feelings of security, and soon displays a sense of attachment to primary caregivers. The newborn:

- Experiences a short period of alertness immediately following birth.
- Sleeps seventeen to nineteen hours a day; is gradually awake and responsive for longer periods.
- Likes to be held close and cuddled when awake.
- Shows qualities of individuality; each infant varies in ways of responding or not responding to similar situations.
- Begins to establish emotional attachment or a **bonding** relationship with parents and caregivers.
- Begins to develop a sense of security or trust with parents and caregivers; responses to different individuals vary. For example, an infant may become tense with a caregiver who is uncomfortable with the infant.

DAILY ROUTINES—BIRTH TO ONE MONTH

Eating

- Takes six to ten feedings, totaling approximately 22 ounces (660 ml) per twenty-four hours at the beginning of this period; later, the number of feedings will decrease to five or six as the amount consumed increases.
- Drinks 2 to 4 ounces of breast milk or formula per feeding; takes twenty-five to thirty minutes to complete a feeding; may fall asleep toward the end.
- Expresses the need for food by crying.
- Should be fed in an upright position to lessen chances of choking and ear infection.

continued

---

bonding—*The establishment of a close, loving relationship between an infant and adult, usually the mother and father; sometimes called attachment.*

Toileting, Bathing, Dressing

- Signals the need for diaper change by crying (if crying does not stop when diaper has been changed, another cause should be sought).
- Enjoys bath; keeps eyes open and gives other indications of pleasure when placed in warm water.
- Expresses displeasure when clothes are pulled over head (best to avoid over-the-head clothes).
- Enjoys being wrapped firmly (swaddled) in a blanket; swaddling seems to foster feelings of security and comfort.
- Has one to four bowel movements per day.

Sleeping

- After the first few days, has four to six sleep periods per twenty-four hours; one of these may be five to seven hours in length.
- Place baby on back or side (propped) on firm mattress to sleep.
- May cry before falling asleep (usually stops if held and rocked briefly).

Play and Social Activities

- Enjoys light and brightness; may fuss if turned away from the light.
- Stares at faces in close visual range (10–12 inches [25.4–30.5 cm]).
- Signals the need for social stimulation by crying; stops when picked up or put in infant seat close to voices and movement.
- Content to lie on back much of the time.
- Before being picked up, needs to be forewarned by first being touched and talked to.
- Enjoys lots of touching and holding; however, may become fussy with over-stimulation.
- Enjoys "en face" (face-to-face) position.

LEARNING ACTIVITIES

Tips for parents and caregivers:

- Respond with gentle and dependable attention to baby's cries so baby learns that help is always available (infants always cry for a reason; crying signals a need).
- Make eye-to-eye contact when baby is in an alert state; make faces or stick out

your tongue, activities that new babies often imitate (imitation is an important avenue for learning).

- Talk or sing to a baby in a normal voice during feeding, diapering, bathing; vary voice tone and rhythm of speech.
- Recognize and show delight in baby's responsiveness. (Mutual responsiveness and social turn-taking are the bases for all teaching and learning in the months and years ahead.)
- Show baby simple pictures (new babies tend to prefer simple drawings of faces); gently move a stuffed animal or toy 10 to 15 inches from baby's face to encourage visual tracking; hang toys or mobile within baby's visual range (change often—novelty increases fascination).
- Take cues from baby; too much stimulation can be as distressing as too little.

DEVELOPMENTAL ALERTS

Check with a health care provider or early childhood specialist if, by one month of age, the infant *does not:*

- Show alarm or "startle" responses to loud noise.
- Suck and swallow with ease.
- Show gains in height, weight, and head circumference.
- Grasp with equal strength in both hands.
- Make eye-to-eye contact when awake and being held.
- Become quiet soon after being picked up.
- Roll head from side to side when placed on stomach.
- Express needs and emotions with cries and patterns of vocalizations that can be distinguished from one another.
- Stop crying when picked up and held.

ONE TO FOUR MONTHS

During these early months, the wonders of infancy continue to unfold. Growth proceeds at a rapid pace. Body systems are fairly well stabilized, with temperature, breathing patterns, and heart rate becoming more regular. Motor skill improves as strength and voluntary muscle control increase. Longer periods of wakefulness encourage the infant's personal-social development. Social responsiveness begins to appear as infants practice and enjoy using their eyes to explore the environment. As social awareness develops, the infant gradually establishes a sense of trust and emotional attachment to parents and caregivers.

While crying remains a primary way of communicating and of gaining adult attention, more complex communication skills are gradually emerging. Infants begin to find great pleasure in imitating the speech sounds and gestures of others. Learning takes place continuously throughout the infant's waking hours as newly acquired skills are used for exploring and gathering information about a still new and unfamiliar environment. However, it is important to note once again that perceptual, cognitive, and motor development are closely interrelated and nearly impossible to differentiate during these early months.

DEVELOPMENT PROFILES AND GROWTH PATTERNS

Growth and Physical Characteristics

- Average length is 20 to 27 inches (50.8–68.6 cm); grows approximately 1 inch (2.54 cm) per month (measured with infant lying on back, from top of the head to bottom of heel, knees straight and foot flexed).
- Weighs an average of 8 to 16 pounds (3.6–7.3 kg); females weigh slightly less than males.
- Gains approximately 1/4 to 1/2 pound per week (0.11–0.22 kg).
- Respiration rate is approximately thirty to forty breaths per minute; rate increases significantly during periods of crying or activity.
- Normal body temperature ranges from 96.4 to 99.6°F (35.7–37.5°C).
- Head and chest circumference are nearly equal.
- Head circumference increases approximately 3/4 inch (1.9 cm) per month until two months, then increases 5/8 inch (1.6 cm) per month until four months. Increases are an important indication of continued brain growth.
- Continues to breathe using abdominal muscles.
- Posterior fontanel closes by the second month.
- Anterior fontanel closes to approximately 1/2 inch (1.3 cm).
- Skin remains sensitive and easily irritated.
- Arms and legs are of equal length, size, and shape; easily flexed and extended.
- Legs may appear slightly bowed.
- Feet appear flat with no arch.
- Cries with tears.
- Eyes begin moving together in unison (binocular vision).
- Color vision is present.

Landau reflex.   Raises up on arms.

Motor Development

- Reflexive motor behaviors are changing:
    —Tonic neck and stepping reflexes disappear.
    —Rooting and sucking reflexes are well developed.
    —Swallowing reflex and tongue movements are still immature; continued drooling and inability to move food to the back of the mouth.
    —Grasp reflex gradually disappears.
    —Landau reflex appears near the middle of this period; when baby is held in a prone (face down) position, the head is held upright and legs are fully extended.
- Grasps with entire hand; strength insufficient to hold items.
- Holds hands in an open or semi-open position.
- Muscle tone and development are equal for boys and girls.
- Muscle strength and control improving; early movements are large and jerky; gradually become smoother and more purposeful.
- Raises head and upper body on arms when in a prone position.
- Turns head side to side when in a supine (face up) position; near the end of this period can hold head up and in line with the body.
- Upper body parts are more active: clasps hands above face, waves arms about, reaches for objects.

Actively plays with hands.

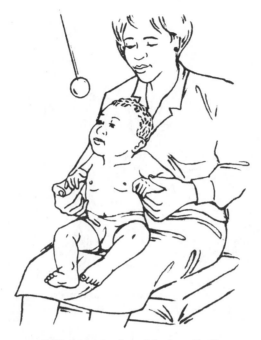

**Follows a moving object vertically
and horizontally.**

- At first, infant rolls from front to back by turning head to one side and allowing trunk to follow. Near the end of this period, infant can roll from front to back to side at will.
- Can be pulled to a sitting position, with considerable head lag and rounded back at the beginning of this period. Later, can be positioned to sit, with minimal head support. By four months, most infants can sit with support, holding their head steady and keeping back fairly erect; enjoys sitting in an infant seat or being held on a lap.

Perceptual-Cognitive Development

- Fixates on a moving object held at a distance of 12 inches (30.5 cm); smoother visual tracking of objects across 180-degree pathway, vertically and horizontally.
- Continues to gaze in direction of moving objects that have disappeared.
- Exhibits some sense of size, color, and shape recognition of objects in the immediate environment—for example, recognizes own bottle even when bottle is turned about, thus presenting a different shape.
- Does not search for a bottle that falls out of a crib or for a toy hidden under a blanket: "out of sight, out of mind."
- Watches hands intently.

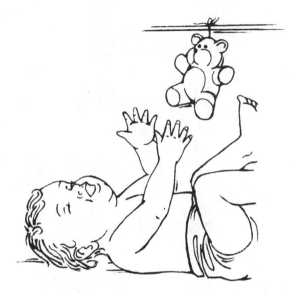

Focuses and reaches for objects.

- Moves eyes from one object to another.
- Focuses on small object and reaches for it; usually follows own hand movements.
- Alternates looking at an object, at one or both hands, and then back at the object.
- Imitates gestures that are modeled: bye-bye, patting head.
- Hits at object closest to right or left hand with some degree of accuracy.
- Looks in the direction of a sound source (sound localization).
- Connects sound and rhythms with movement by moving or jiggling in time to music, singing, or chanting.
- Can distinguish parent's face from stranger's face when other cues, such as voice, touch, or smell are also available.
- Attempts to keep toy in motion by repeating arm or leg movements that started the toy moving in the first place.
- Begins to mouth objects.

Speech and Language Development

- Initially, the infant reacts (stops whimpering, startles) to sounds, such as a voice, rattle or bell. Later, will search for sound source by turning head and moving eyes.
- Coordinates vocalizing, looking, and body movements in face-to-face exchanges with parent or caregiver; can follow and lead in keeping communication going.
- Babbles or coos when spoken to or smiled at.

Turns toward sound.

- Coos using single vowel sounds (*ah, eh, uh*); also imitates own sounds and vowel sounds produced by others.
- Laughs out loud.

Personal-Social Development

- Can imitate, maintain, terminate, and avoid interactions—for example, infant turns at will toward or away from a person or situation.
- Reacts differently to variations in adult voices; for example, may frown or look anxious if voices are loud, angry, or unfamiliar.
- Enjoys being held and cuddled at times other than feeding and bedtime.

Responds with a social smile.

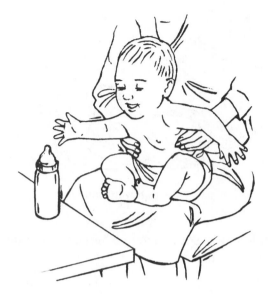

Recognizes and enjoys familiar routines.

- Coos, gurgles, and squeals when awake.
- Smiles in response to a friendly face or voice; smiles occurring during sleep are thought to be reflexive.
- Can entertain self by playing with fingers, hands, and toes.
- Enjoys familiar routines, such as being bathed and having diaper changed.
- Delights in play that involves gentle tickling, laughing, and jiggling.
- Spends much less time crying.
- Recognizes and reaches out to familiar faces and objects, such as father or bottle; reacts by waving arms and squealing with excitement.
- Stops crying when parent or caregiver comes near.

DAILY ROUTINES—ONE TO FOUR MONTHS

Eating

- Takes five to eight feedings, each 5 to 6 ounces per day.
- Begins fussing before anticipated feeding times; does not always cry to signal the need to eat.
- Needs only a little assistance in getting nipple to mouth; beginning to help by using own hands to guide nipple.

continued

- Sucks vigorously; may choke on occasion because of the vigor and enthusiasm of sucking.
- Becomes impatient if bottle or breast continues to be offered once hunger is satisfied.
- Not ready to eat solid foods.

Toileting, Bathing, Dressing

- Usually enjoys bathtime; kicks, laughs, and splashes.
- Has one or two bowel movements per day; frequently skips a day.
- Beginning to establish a regular time or pattern for bowel movements.

Sleeping

- Often falls asleep for the night soon after the evening feeding.
- Begins to sleep through the night; many babies do not sleep more than six hours at a stretch for several more months.
- Averages fourteen to seventeen hours of sleep per day; often awake for two or three periods during the daytime.
- Thumbsucking may begin during this period.
- Begins to entertain self before falling asleep: "talks," plays with hands, jiggles crib.

Play and Social Activity

- Spends waking periods in physical activity: kicking, turning head from side to side, clasping hands together, grasping objects.
- Becoming "talkative"; vocalizes with delight.
- Likes being talked and sung to; may cry when the social interaction ends.
- Appears happy when awake and alone (for short periods of time).

LEARNING ACTIVITIES

Tips for parents and caregivers:

- Imitate baby's vocalizations and faces (grunting, smacking, yawning, squinting, frowning). When baby begins to smile, smile back and sometimes remark, "You are smiling! Nice smile!"

- Sing songs and read to baby out of magazines, books, whatever interests you; it's the sound of your voice and your closeness that matter.
- Play simplified peek-a-boo (hold cloth in front of your own face, drop it, say *peek-a-boo*); repeat if baby shows interest.
- Gently stretch and bend baby's arms and legs while making up an accompanying song; later, start a gentle "bicycling" activity.
- Touch baby's hand with a small toy* (soft rattles or other noisemakers are especially good); encourage baby to grasp toy.
- Walk around with baby, touching and naming objects. Stand with baby in front of mirror, touching and naming facial features: "Baby's mouth, Daddy's mouth. Baby's eye, Mommy's eye."
- Attach an unbreakable mirror to crib or wall close to the crib so baby can look and talk to himself or herself.
- Fasten (*securely*) small bells to baby's booties; this helps baby to localize sounds and learn, at the same time, that he or she has power and can make things happen simply by moving about.

Toys and other objects given to an infant should be no smaller than the baby's fist in order to prevent choking or swallowing.

DEVELOPMENTAL ALERTS

Check with a health care provider or early childhood specialist if, by four months of age, the infant *does not:*

- Continue to show steady increases in height, weight, and head circumference.
- Smile in response to the smiles of others (the social smile is a significant developmental milestone).
- Follow a moving object with eyes focusing together.
- Bring hands together over midchest.
- Turn head to locate sounds.
- Begin to raise head and upper body when placed on stomach.
- Reach for objects or familiar persons.

FOUR TO EIGHT MONTHS

Between four and eight months, infants are developing a wide range of skills and greater ability to use their bodies. Infants seem to be busy every waking moment. They manipulate and mouth toys and other objects that come to hand. They "talk" all the time, making vowel and consonant sounds in ever greater variety and complexity. They initiate social interactions and respond to all kinds of cues, such as facial expressions, gestures, and the comings and goings of everyone in their world. Infants at this age are both self-contained and sociable. They move easily from spontaneous, self-initiated activity to social activities initiated by others.

DEVELOPMENTAL PROFILES AND GROWTH PATTERNS

Growth and Physical Characteristics

- Gains approximately 1 pound (2.2 kg) per month in weight.
- Doubles original birth weight.
- Gains approximately 1/2 inch (1.3 cm) in length per month; average length is 27.5 to 29 inches (69.8–73.7 cm).
- Head and chest circumferences are nearly equal.
- Head circumference increases approximately 3/8 inch (0.95 cm) per month until six to seven months, then 3/16 inch (0.47 cm) per month; head circumference should continue to increase steadily, indicating healthy, ongoing brain growth.
- Breathing is abdominal; ranges from twenty-five to fifty breaths per minute, depending on activity; rate and patterns vary from infant to infant.
- Teeth begin to appear, with upper and lower incisors coming in first. Gums may become red and swollen, accompanied by increased drooling, chewing, biting, and mouthing of objects.

Chews and mouths objects.

4–8 MONTHS

Parachute reflex.

- Legs may appear bowed; bowing gradually disappears as infant grows older.
- True eye color is established.

Motor Development

- Reflexive behaviors are changing:
    —Blinking reflex is well established
    —Sucking reflex becomes voluntary
    —Moro reflex disappears
    —Parachute reflex appears toward the end of this stage (when held in a prone, horizontal position and lowered suddenly, infant throws out arms as a protective measure).
    —Swallowing reflex appears (a more complex form of swallowing that involves tongue movement against the roof of mouth); allows infant to move solid foods from front of mouth to the back for swallowing.
- Uses finger and thumb (pincer grip) to pick up objects.
- Reaches for objects with both arms simultaneously; later reaches with one hand or the other.
- Transfers objects from one hand to the other; grasps object using entire hand (palmar grasp).
- Handles, shakes, and pounds objects; puts everything in mouth.
- Holds own bottle.

Transfers objects from one hand to the other.

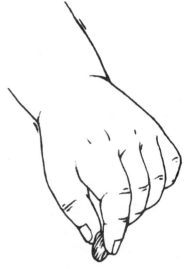

Pincer grasp.

- Sits alone without support, holding head erect, back straightened, and arms propped forward for support.
- Pulls self into a crawling position by raising up on arms and drawing knees up beneath the body; rocks back and forth, but generally does not move forward.
- Lifts head when placed on back.
- Rolls over from front to back and back to front.
- May accidentally begin scooting backwards when placed on stomach; soon will begin to crawl forward.
- Enjoys being placed in standing position, especially on someone's lap; jumps in place.

Palmar grasp.

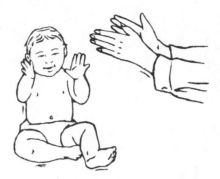

Plays pat-a-cake.

Perceptual-Cognitive Development

- Turns toward and locates familiar voices and sounds: this behavior can be used to informally test an infant's hearing.
- Focuses eyes on small objects and reaches for them.
- Uses hand, mouth, and eyes in coordination to explore own body, toys, and surroundings.
- Imitates actions, such as pat-a-cake, waving bye-bye, and playing peek-a-boo.
- Shows fear of falling off high places, such as changing table, stairs; **depth perception** is clearly evident.
- Looks over side of crib or high chair for objects dropped; delights in repeatedly throwing objects overboard for caregiver to retrieve.

Inspects objects with eyes and hands.

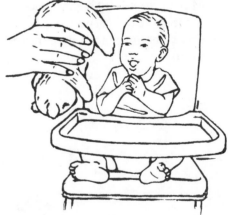

Recognizes inverted but familiar objects.

---

depth perception—*Ability to determine the relative distance of objects from the observer.*

- Searches for toy or food that has been completely hidden under cloth or behind screen; beginning to understand that objects continue to exist even when they cannot be seen. (Piaget refers to this as **"object permanence."**)
- Handles and explores objects in a variety of ways: visually; turning them around; feeling all surfaces; banging and shaking.
- Picks up inverted object (in other words, recognizes a cup even when it is positioned differently).
- Unable to deal with more than one toy at a time; may either ignore second toy or drop toy in one hand in order to focus vision on the new toy.
- Reaches accurately with either hand.
- Plays actively with small toys, such as rattle or block.
- Bangs objects together playfully; bangs spoon on table.
- Continues to put everything in mouth.
- Establishes full attachment to mother or single caregiver which coincides with growing understanding of object permanence.

Speech and Language Development

- Responds appropriately to own name and simple requests, such as "eat," "wave bye-bye."

Responds to own name.

object permanence—*Piaget's sensorimotor stage when infants understand that an object exists even when not in sight.*

Turns to watch people and activities.

- Imitates some nonspeech sounds, such as cough, tongue click, lip smacking.
- Produces a full range of vowels and some consonants: *r, s, z, th,* and *w.*
- Responds to variations in the tone of voice of others—anger, playfulness, sadness.
- Expresses emotions, such as pleasure, satisfaction, and anger, by making different sounds.
- "Talks" to toys.
- Babbles by repeating same syllable in a series: *ba, ba, ba.*

Still friendly with strangers.

- Reacts differently to noises, such as a vacuum cleaner, phone ringing, or dog barking; may cry, whimper, or look for reassurance from parent or caregiver.

Personal-Social Development

- Delights in observing surroundings; continuously watches people and activities.
- Developing an awareness of self as a separate individual from others.
- Becomes more outgoing and social in nature: smiles, coos, reaches out.
- Can tell the difference between, and responds differently, to strangers, caretakers, parents, and siblings.
- Responds differently and appropriately to facial expressions: frowns; smiles.
- Imitates facial expressions, actions, and sounds.
- Still friendly toward strangers at the beginning of this stage; later, is reluctant to be approached by, or left with, strangers; exhibits "**stranger anxiety.**"
- Enjoys being held and cuddled; indicates desire to be picked up by raising arms.
- Establishes a trust relationship with parents and caregivers if physical and emotional needs are met consistently; by six months, begins to show preference for primary caregiver.
- Laughs out loud.
- Becomes upset if toy or other objects are taken away.
- Seeks attention by using body movements, verbalizations, or both.

DAILY ROUTINES—FOUR TO EIGHT MONTHS

Eating

- Adjusts feeding times to the family's schedule; usually takes three or four feedings per day, each 6 to 8 ounces, depending on sleep schedule.
- Shows interest in feeding activities; reaches for cup and spoon while being fed.
- Able to wait half hour or more after awakening for first morning feeding.
- Has less need for sucking.
- Begins to accept small amount of solid foods, such as cereal and vegetables when placed well back on tongue (if placed on tip, infant will push it back out).
- Closes mouth firmly or turns head away when hunger is satisfied.

continued

stranger anxiety—Distress or fear shown when approached by unfamiliar persons.

Toileting, Bathing, Dressing

- Enjoys being free of clothes.
- Splashes vigorously with both hands and sometimes feet during bathtime.
- Moves hands constantly; nothing within reach is safe from being spilled, placed in the mouth, or dashed to the floor.
- Pulls off own socks; plays with strings, buttons, and velcro closures on clothing.
- Has one bowel movement per day as a general rule.
- Urinates often and in quantity; female infants tend to have longer intervals between wetting.

Sleeping

- Awakens between 6 and 8 A.M.; usually falls asleep soon after evening meal.
- No longer wakens for a late-night feeding.
- Sleeps eleven to thirteen hours through the night.
- Takes two or three naps per day (however, there is great variability among infants).

Play and Social Activity

- Enjoys lying on back; arches back, kicks, stretches legs upwards, grasps feet and brings them to mouth.
- Looks at own hands with interest and delight; may squeal or gaze at them intently.
- Enjoys playing with soft, squeaky toys and rattles; puts them in mouth, bites, and chews on them.
- "Talks" happily to self: gurgles, growls, makes high squealing sounds.
- Differentiates between people: lively with those who are familiar, anxious about, or ignores, others.
- Likes rhythmic activities: being bounced, jiggled, swayed about gently.

LEARNING ACTIVITIES

Tips for parents and caregivers:

- Gradually elaborate on earlier activities: imitate baby's sounds, facial expressions, and body movements; name body parts; look in the mirror together and make faces; read, talk, and sing to baby throughout the day.

- Use baby's name during all kinds of activities so baby comes to recognize it: "*Kyle* is smiling," "*Carla's* eyes are wide open."
- Provide toys, rattles, and household items that make noise as baby shakes or waves them (a set of measuring spoons or plastic keys, shaker cans, squeak toys; remember the "*Rule of fist,*" p. 52.)
- Fasten a cradle gym across the crib; a younger baby can swipe at objects and later actually connect (both activities are essential in learning eye–hand coordination). Homemade cradle gyms made of safe household items are equally effective.
- Play and move to radio or taped music with baby; vary the tempo and movement: gentle jiggling, dancing, turning in circles; dance in front of the mirror, describing movements to baby.
- Allow plenty of time for bathtime. This activity provides an important opportunity for learning in all developmental areas, as well as an overall enjoyment of learning.
- Play *This little piggy, Where's baby's* (nose, eye, hand . . .), and other simple games invented on the spot, such as taking turns at shaking rattles or gently rubbing foreheads.

4–8 MONTHS

DEVELOPMENTAL ALERTS

Check with a health care provider or early childhood specialist if, by eight months of age, the infant *does not:*

- Show even, steady increase in weight, height, and head size (too slow or too rapid growth are both causes for concern).
- Explore own hands and objects placed in hands.
- Hold and shake a rattle.
- Smile, babble, and laugh out loud.
- Search for hidden objects.
- Use pincer grasp to pick up objects.
- Have an interest in playing games, such as "pat-a-cake" and "peek-a-boo."
- Appear interested in new or unusual sounds.
- Reach for and grasp objects.
- Sit alone.
- Begin to eat some solid foods.

EIGHT TO TWELVE MONTHS

Between eight months and one year of age, the infant is gearing up for two major developmental events—walking and talking. These milestones usually begin about the time of the first birthday. The infant is increasingly able to manipulate small objects, and spends a great deal of time practicing by picking up and releasing toys or whatever else is at hand. Infants at this age are also becoming extremely sociable. They find ways to be the center of attention and to win approval and applause from family and friends. When applause is forthcoming, the infant joins in with delight. The ability to imitate improves and serves two purposes: to extend social interactions and to help the child learn many new skills and behaviors in the months of rapid development that lie ahead.

DEVELOPMENTAL PROFILES AND GROWTH PATTERNS

Growth and Physical Characteristics

- Gains in height are slower than during the previous months, averaging 1/2 inch (1.3 cm) per month. Infants reach approximately 1-1/2 times their birth length by the first birthday.

Pulls self to standing position.

- Weight increases by approximately 1 pound (0.5 kg) per month; birth weight nearly triples by one year of age: infants weigh an average of 21 pounds (9.6 kg).
- Respiration rates vary with activity: typically, twenty to forty-five breaths per minute.
- Body temperature ranges from 96.4°F to 99.6°F (35.7–37.5°C); environmental conditions, weather, activity, and clothing still affect variations in temperature.
- Head and chest circumference remain equal.
- Continues to use abdominal muscles for breathing.
- Anterior fontanel begins to close.
- Approximately four upper and four lower incisors and two lower molars erupt.
- Arm and hands are more developed than feet and legs (cephalocaudal development); hands appear large in proportion to other body parts.
- Legs may continue to appear bowed.
- Feet appear flat as arch has not yet fully developed.
- Visual acuity is approximately 20/100.
- Both eyes work in unison (true binocular coordination).
- Can see distant objects (15 to 20 feet away) and points at them.

Motor Development

- Reaches with one hand leading to grasp an offered object or toy.
- Manipulates objects, transferring them from one hand to the other.
- Explores new objects by poking with one finger.
- Uses deliberate pincer grasp to pick up small objects, toys, and finger foods.
- Stacks objects; also places objects inside one another.
- Releases objects or toys by dropping or throwing; cannot intentionally put an object down.
- Beginning to pull self to a standing position.
- Beginning to stand alone, leaning on furniture for support; moves around obstacles by side-stepping.
- Has good balance when sitting; can shift positions without falling.
- Creeps on hands and knees; crawls up and down stairs.
- Walks with adult support, holding onto adult's hand; may begin to walk alone.

Perceptual-Cognitive Development

- Watches people, objects, and activities in the immediate environment.
- Shows awareness of distant objects (15 to 20 feet away) by pointing at them.
- Responds to hearing tests (voice localization); however, loses interest quickly and, therefore, may be difficult to test informally.
- Follows simple instructions.

Walks with adult support.

- Reaches for toys that are out of reach but visible.
- Still puts everything in mouth.
- Continues to drop first item when other toys or items are offered.
- Recognizes the reversal of an object: cup upside down is still a cup.
- Imitates activities: hitting two blocks together, playing pat-a-cake.
- Drops toys intentionally and repeatedly; looks in direction of fallen object.

**Continues to put everything
in the mouth.**

- Shows appropriate use of everyday items: pretends to drink from cup, put on necklace, hug doll, make stuffed animal "walk."
- Shows some sense of spatial relationships: puts block in cup and takes it out when requested to do so.
- Beginning to show an understanding of causality—for example, hands mechanical toy back to adult to have it rewound.
- Shows some awareness of the working relationship of objects; puts spoon in mouth, uses brush to smooth hair, turns pages of a book.
- Searches for partially hidden toy by the end of this period.

Speech and Language Development

- Babbles or jabbers deliberately to get a social interaction started; may shout to attract attention; listens, then shouts again.
- Shakes head for "no" and may nod for "yes."
- Responds by looking for voice when name is called.
- Babbling in sentence-like sequences; followed later by jargon (syllables and sounds with language-like inflection).
- Waves "bye-bye"; claps hands when asked.
- Says "da-da" and "ma-ma."

Understands the use of everyday objects.

Resists separating from parent.

8–12 MONTHS

- Imitates sounds that are similar to those the baby has already learned to make; will also imitate motor noises, tongue click, lip smacking, coughing.
- Enjoys rhymes and simple songs; vocalizes and dances to music.
- Hands toy or object to an adult when appropriate gestures accompany the request.

Personal-Social Development

- Exhibits a definite fear of strangers; clings to, or hides behind, parent or caregiver ("stranger anxiety"); often resists separating from familiar adult ("separation anxiety").
- Wants parent or caregiver to be in constant sight.
- Sociable and outgoing; enjoys being near, and included in, daily activities of family members and caregivers.
- Enjoys novel experiences and opportunities to examine new objects.
- Shows need to be picked up and held by extending arms upward, crying, or clinging to adult's legs.
- Begins to exhibit assertiveness by resisting caregiver's requests; may kick, scream, or throw self on the floor.
- Offers toys and objects to others.
- Often becomes attached to a favorite toy or blanket.
- Upon hearing own name, looks up and smiles at person who is speaking.
- Repeats behaviors that get attention; jabbers continuously.
- Carries out simple directions and requests; understands the meaning of "no."

DAILY ROUTINES—EIGHT TO TWELVE MONTHS

Eating

- Eats three meals a day plus midmorning or midafternoon snacks, such as juice and crackers.
- Begins to refuse bottle (if this has not already occurred).
- Has good appetite.
- Enjoys drinking from a cup; holds own cup; will even tilt head backward to get the last drop.
- Begins to eat finger foods; may remove food from mouth, look at it, put it back in.
- Develops certain likes and dislikes for foods.

continued

8–12 MONTHS

- Continuously active; infant's hands may be so busy that a toy is needed for each hand in order to prevent cup or dish from being turned over or food grabbed and tossed.

Toileting, Bathing, Dressing

- Enjoys bathtime; plays with washcloth, soap, and water toys.
- Loves to let water drip from sponge or washcloth.
- Shows great interest in pulling off hats, taking off shoes and socks.
- Fusses when diaper needs changing; may pull off soiled or wet diaper.
- Cooperates to some degree in being dressed; helps put arm in armholes, may even extend legs to have pants put on.
- Has one or two bowel movements per day.
- Occasionally dry after nap.

Sleeping

- Willing to go to bed; may not fall asleep immediately, but will play or walk about in crib, then fall asleep on top of covers.
- Sleeps until 6 or 8 A.M.
- Plays alone and quietly for fifteen to thirty minutes after awakening; then begins to make demanding noises, signaling the need to be up and about.
- Plays actively in crib when awake; crib sides must be up and securely fastened.
- Takes one afternoon nap most days.

Play and Social Activities

- Enjoys large motor activities: pulling to stand, cruising, standing alone, creeping. Some babies are walking at this point.
- Enjoys putting things on head: basket, bowl, cup; finds this very funny and expects people to notice and laugh.
- Puts objects in and out of each other: pans that nest, toys in and out of a box.
- Enjoys hiding behind chairs to play "Where's baby?"
- Throws things on floor and expects them to be returned.
- Shows interest in opening and closing doors and cupboards.
- Gives an object to adult on request; expects to have it returned immediately.
- Responds to "no-no" by stopping; on the other hand, the infant may smile, laugh, and continue inappropriate behavior, thus making a game out of it.

8–12 MONTHS

LEARNING ACTIVITIES

Tips for parents and caregivers:

- Elaborate on activities suggested earlier; always pick up on baby's lead whenever baby initiates a new response or invents a new version of a familiar game (the roots of creativity).
- Provide safe floor space close to parent or caregiver; learning to sit, crawl, stand, and explore are a baby's major tasks during these months.
- Read and tell short stories about everyday happenings in baby's life; also read from sturdy, brightly colored picture books, allowing baby to help turn the pages.
- Talk about ongoing activities, emphasizing key words: "Here is the *soap*," "You are *squeezing* the sponge."
- Give baby simple instructions: "Pat Mommy's head," "Pat baby's head." Allow adequate time for response; if baby seems interested, but does not respond, demonstrate the response.
- Accept baby's newly invented game of dropping things off highchair or tray or out of the crib; it's baby's way of learning about many things: cause and effect, gravity, adults' patience.
- Provide containers that baby can fill with small toys or other objects and then empty out. ("Rule of fist" still applies.)
- Give baby push and pull toys, roly-polies, toys with wheels. (Helping unpack canned goods and rolled them across the kitchen floor is an all-time favorite game.)

DEVELOPMENTAL ALERTS

Check with a health care provider or early childhood specialist if, by twelve months of age, the infant *does not:*

- Blink when fast-moving objects approach the eyes.
- Begin to cut teeth.

- Imitate simple sounds.
- Follow simple verbal requests: *come, bye-bye.*
- Pull self to a standing position.
- Transfer objects from hand to hand.
- Show anxiety toward strangers.
- Interact playfully with parents, caregivers, and siblings.
- Feed self; hold own bottle or cup; pick up and eat finger foods.
- Creep or crawl on hands and knees.

Test Your Knowledge

REVIEW QUESTIONS

1. List three physical characteristics of the newborn.

   a.

   b.

   c.

2. List three ways in which it is possible to informally evaluate hearing in an infant who is not yet talking.

   a.

   b.

   c.

3. List three reflexes present in the newborn that should disappear by the time the infant is a year old.

   a.

   b.

   c.

4. List three perceptual-cognitive skills that appear during the first year of life.

   a.

   b.

   c.

TRUE OR FALSE

1. Newborns are incapable of learning until they can stay awake for more than an hour or two at a time.

2. The newborn will startle in response to a loud noise.

3. Crying serves no useful developmental function except to let the infant signal hunger, a need to be changed, or to be covered more warmly.

4. An infant's head circumference is measured regularly in order to assess brain growth.

5. Imitation should be discouraged in infants to ensure that they will not grow up to be "copycats."

6. The healthy infant has nearly tripled its birth weight by one year of age.

7. All normally developing infants crawl on all fours before they walk.

8. The six-month-old who keeps throwing toys out of the crib should be scolded for causing extra work for the parent or caregiver.

9. Developmentally, there is no excuse for nine- or ten-month-old children to be afraid of strangers unless they have previously had a bad experience.

MULTIPLE CHOICE   *Select one item in each of the following groupings that is* not *typically observed in the majority of infants for the age category listed.*

1. Birth to one month

   a. cries without tears.

   b. synchronizes body movements to speech patterns of parent or caregiver.

   c. shows need to be picked up by extending arms.

2. One to four months

   a. waves bye-bye, plays pat-a-cake on request.

   b. babbles or coos when spoken to or smiled at.

   c. TNR and stepping reflex disappear.

3. Four to eight months

   a. shows full attachment to mother or primary caregiver.

   b. expresses emotions, such as pleasure, anger, and distress by making different kinds of sounds.

   c. sees outlines and shapes of nearby objects, but cannot focus on distant objects.

4. Eight months to one year
   a. usually sleeps through the night.
   b. cuts several teeth.
   c. has a vocabulary of at least fifty words.

THE TODDLER

TWELVE TO TWENTY-FOUR MONTHS

The toddler is a dynamo, full of unlimited energy, enthusiasm, and curiosity. While the rate of growth slows considerably during this stage, important developmental changes are taking place. The toddler begins this period with the limited abilities of an infant and ends with the relatively sophisticated skills of a young child.

Improvements in motor skills allow toddlers to move about on their own, to explore, and to test their surroundings. Rapid development of speech and language contributes to more complex thinking and learning abilities. Defiance and negative responses become commonplace near the end of this stage. Gradually, the toddler begins to assert independence as a way of gaining autonomy (a sense of self as separate and self-managed) and some degree of control over parents and caregivers.

THE ONE-YEAR-OLD

The ability to stand upright and toddle from place to place enables one-year-olds to gain new insight about their surroundings. They become talkers and doers, stopping only for much-needed meals and bedtimes. Their curiosity mounts, their skills become increasingly advanced, and their energy level seems never-ending. One-year-olds believe that everything and everyone exists for their benefit. Eventually, this egocentricity, or self-centeredness, gives way to a greater respect for others. However, for now, the one-year-old is satisfied to declare everything "mine" and to imitate the play and actions of other children rather than join in.

DEVELOPMENTAL PROFILES AND GROWTH PATTERNS

Growth and Physical Characteristics

- Rate of growth is considerably slower during this period.
- Height increases approximately 2 to 3 inches (5.0–7.6 cm) per year; toddlers reach an average height of 32 to 35 inches (81.3–88.9 cm).

Stands upright with support.

- Weighs approximately 21 to 27 pounds (9.6–12.3 kg); gains 1/4 to 1/2 pound (0.13–0.25 kg) per month; weight is now approximately 3 times the child's birth weight.
- Respiration rate is typically twenty-two to thirty breaths per minute; varies with emotional state and activity.
- Heart rate (pulse) is approximately 80 to 110 per minute.
- Head size increases slowly; grows approximately 1/2 inch (1.3 cm) every six months; anterior fontanel is nearly closed at eighteen months as bones of the skull thicken.
- Chest circumference is larger than head circumference.
- Rapid eruption of teeth; six to ten new teeth will appear.
- Legs may still appear bowed.
- Body shape changes; takes on more adult-like appearance; still appears top-heavy; abdomen protrudes, back is swayed.
- Visual acuity is approximately 20/60.

Motor Development

- Crawls skillfully and quickly.
- Stands alone with feet spread apart, legs stiffened, and arms extended for support.
- Gets to feet unaided.
- Most children walk unassisted near the end of this period; falls often; not always able to maneuver around obstacles, such as furniture or toys.

12–24 MONTHS

- Uses furniture to lower self to floor; collapses backwards into a sitting position or falls forward on hands and then sits.
- Voluntarily releases an object.
- Enjoys pushing or pulling toys while walking.
- Repeatedly picks up objects and throws them; direction becomes more deliberate.
- Attempts to run; has difficulty stopping and usually just drops to the floor.
- Crawls up stairs on all fours; goes down stairs in same position.
- Sits in a small chair.
- Carries toys from place to place.
- Enjoys crayons and markers for scribbling; uses whole-arm movement.
- Helps feed self; enjoys holding spoon (often upside down) and drinking from a glass or cup; not always accurate in getting utensils into mouth; frequent spills should be expected.
- Helps turn pages in book.
- Stacks two to four objects.

Perceptual-Cognitive Development

- Enjoys object-hiding activities:
  —Early in this period, the child always searches in the same location for a hidden object (if the child has watched the hiding of an object). Later, the child will search in several locations.
- Passes toy to other hand when offered a second object (referred to as "crossing the midline"—an important neurological development).
- Manages three to four objects by setting an object aside (on lap or floor) when presented with a new toy.
- Puts toys in mouth less often.

12–24 MONTHS

**Enjoys sharing picture books
with adults.**

- Enjoys looking at picture books.
- Demonstrates understanding of functional relationships (objects that belong together):
    —Puts spoon in bowl and then uses spoon as if eating.
    —Places cup on saucer and sips from cup.
    —Tries to make doll stand up.
- Shows or offers toy to another person to look at.
- Names many everyday objects.
- Shows increasing understanding of spatial and form discrimination: puts all pegs in a pegboard; places three geometric shapes in large formboard or puzzle.
- Places several small items (blocks, clothespins, cereal pieces) in a container or bottle and then dumps them out.
- Tries to make mechanical objects work after watching someone else do so.
- Responds with some facial movement, but cannot truly imitate facial expression.

Speech and Language Development

- Produces considerable "jargon": puts words and sounds together into speech-like (inflected) patterns.
- Holophrastic speech: uses one word to convey an entire thought; meaning depends on the inflection ("me" may be used to request more cookies or a desire to feed self). Later, produces two-word phrases to express a complete thought (telegraphic speech): "More cookie," "Daddy bye-bye."
- Follows simple directions, "Give Daddy the cup."
- When asked, will point to familiar persons, animals, and toys.
- Identifies three body parts if someone names them: "Show me your nose (toe, ear)."
- Indicates a few desired objects and activities by name: "Bye-bye," "cookie"; verbal request is often accompanied by an insistent gesture.
- Responds to simple questions with "yes" or "no" and appropriate head movement.
- Speech is 25 to 50 percent **intelligible** during this period.
- Locates familiar objects on request (if child knows location of objects).
- Acquires and uses five to fifty words; typically these are words that refer to animals, food, and toys.
- Uses gestures, such as pointing or pulling, to direct adult attention.
- Enjoys rhymes and songs; tries to join in.
- Seems aware of reciprocal (back and forth) aspects of conversational exchanges; some turn-taking in other kinds of vocal exchanges, such as making and imitating sounds.

12–24 MONTHS

---

intelligible—Language that can be understood by others.

"Where's mommy's nose?"

"Me baby"

Personal-Social Development

- Usually friendly toward others; less wary of strangers.
- Helps pick up and put away toys.
- Plays alone for short periods.
- Enjoys being held and read to.
- Often imitates adult actions in play.
- Enjoys adult attention; likes to know that an adult is near; gives hugs and kisses.
- Recognizes self in mirror.
- Enjoys the companionship of other children, but does not play cooperatively.
- Beginning to assert independence; often refuses to cooperate with daily routines that once were enjoyable; resists getting dressed, putting on shoes, eating, taking a bath; wants to try doing things without help.
- May have a tantrum when things go wrong or if overly tired or frustrated.
- Exceedingly curious about people and surroundings; toddlers need to be watched carefully to prevent them from getting into unsafe situations.

DAILY ROUTINES—TWELVE TO TWENTY-FOUR MONTHS

Eating

- Has smaller appetite; lunch is often the preferred meal.
- Sometimes described as a finicky or fussy eater; may go on "food jags" (willingness to eat only a few foods); neither requires, nor wants, a large amount of food.

continued

- Occasionally holds food in mouth without swallowing it; usually indicates child does not need or want any more to eat.
- Uses spoon with some degree of skill (if hungry and interested in eating).
- Has good control of cup: lifts it up, drinks from it, sets it down, holds it with one hand.
- Helps feed self; some toddlers this age can feed themselves independently; others still need help.

Toileting, Bathing, Dressing

- Tries to wash self; plays with washcloth and soap.
- Helps with dressing: puts arm in sleeve, lifts feet to have socks put on. Likes to dress and undress self: takes off own shoes and stockings; often puts shirt on upside down and backwards or both feet in one pant leg.
- Lets parent or caregiver know when diaper or pants are soiled or wet.
- Begins to gain some control of bowels and bladder; complete control often not achieved until around age three.

Sleeping

- Falls asleep around 8 or 9 P.M.; however, will often fall asleep at dinner if nap has been missed. Sleeps through the night ten to twelve hours.
- May have problems falling sleep; overflow of energy shows itself in bouncing and jumping, calling for mother, demanding a drink or trip to the bathroom, singing, making and remaking bed—all of which seem to be ways of "winding down." A short bedtime routine can help child prepare for sleep.
- Makes many requests at bedtime for stuffed toys, book or two, a special blanket.

Play and Social Activity

- Develops a strong sense of property rights; "mine" is heard frequently. Sharing is difficult; hoards toys and other items.
- Enjoys helping, but gets into "trouble" when left alone: smears toothpaste, tries on lipstick, empties dresser drawers.
- Enjoys talking about pictures; likes repetition, as in *Drummer Hoff, Mr. Bear,* and *Dr. Seuss* books.
- Enjoys walks; stops frequently to look at things (rocks, gum wrappers, insects); squats to examine and pick up objects; much dawdling with no real interest in getting any place in particular.

12–24 MONTHS

continued

- Still plays alone (solitary play) most of the time, though showing some interest in other children; lots of watching. Some occasional parallel play (play alongside, but not with another child), but no cooperative play as of yet (exception may be children who have spent considerable time in group care).
- At bedtime needs door left slightly ajar with light on in another room; seems to feel more secure, better able to settle down.
- Continues to nap; naps too long or too late will interfere with bedtime.
- Wakes up slowly from nap; cannot be hurried or rushed into any activity.

LEARNING ACTIVITIES

Tips for parents and caregivers:

- Respond to the toddler's jabbering and voice inflections, both in kind (playfully) and with simple words; maintain a conversational turn-taking.
- Encourage the toddler to point to familiar objects in picture books, catalogues, and magazines; name the objects and encourage (do not insist) the toddler to imitate.
- Hide a toy or other familiar object in an obvious place and encourage the toddler to find it (give clues as needed).
- Provide blocks, stacking rings, shape-sorting boxes, nesting cups; such toys promote problem solving and eye–hand coordination.
- Allow frequent water play; the sink is always a favorite when an adult is working in the kitchen. (An old, absorbent throw rug will catch spills and drips, thus reducing the chances of slipping or falling.)
- Put favorite toys in different parts of the room so the toddler must get to them by crawling, cruising, or walking (thus practicing motor skills).
- Provide toys that can be pushed or pulled, a stable plastic or wooden riding toy to steer and propel with the feet; arrange safe, low places for climbing over, under, and on top of.

DEVELOPMENTAL ALERTS

Check with a health care provider or early childhood specialist if, by twenty-four months of age, the child *does not*:

- Attempt to talk or repeat words.
- Understand some new words.
- Respond to simple questions with "yes" or "no."
- Walk alone (or with very little help).
- Exhibit a variety of emotions: anger, delight, fear.
- Show interest in pictures.
- Recognize self in mirror.
- Attempt self-feeding: hold own cup to mouth and drink.

THE TWO-YEAR-OLD

This year can be a challenge—for the child, as well as for caregivers. Exasperated adults typically describe a two-year-old as "impossible" (or demanding, unreasonable, contrary). However, the two-year-old's fierce determination, tantrums, and inability to accept limits are part of normal development and seldom under the child's control. The two-year-old faces demands that can be overwhelming: new skills and behaviors to be learned and remembered, learned responses to be perfected, and puzzling adult expectations with which to comply. Also, conflicting feelings of dependence and independence (autonomy) must be resolved. Is it any wonder that two-year-olds are frustrated, have difficulty making choices, and say no even to things they really want?

While this transitional year can be trying for all, good things also happen. Two-year-olds are noted for their frequent and spontaneous bursts of laughter and affection. Also, as new skills are acquired and earlier learning are consolidated, the two-year-old gradually begins to function more ably and amiably.

DEVELOPMENTAL PROFILES AND GROWTH PATTERNS

Growth and Physical Development

- Weight gain averages 2 to 2.5 pounds (0.9–1.1 kg) per year; weighs approximately 26 to 32 pounds (11.8–14.5 kg) or about 4 times the weight at birth.
- Grows approximately 3 to 5 inches (7.6–12.7 cm) per year; average height is 34 to 38 inches (86.3–96.5 cm).
- Posture is more erect; abdomen still large and protruding, back swayed, because abdominal muscles are not yet fully developed.
- Respirations are slow and regular (approximately twenty to thirty-five breaths per minute).
- Body temperature continues to fluctuate with activity, emotional state, and environment.
- Brain reaches about 80 percent of its adult size.

2-YEAR-OLDS

**Tries hard to balance on
one foot.**

- Eruption of teeth is nearly complete; second molars appear, for a total of twenty deciduous or "baby" teeth.

Motor Development

- Wide-stanced walk giving way to more erect, heel-to-toe pattern; able to maneuver around obstacles in pathway.
- Runs with greater confidence; has fewer falls.

Works at opening doors.

- Squats for long periods while playing.
- Climbs stairs unassisted (but not with alternating feet).
- Balances on one foot (for a few moments), jumps up and down, but may fall.
- Often achieves toilet training during this year (depending on child's physical and neurological development) although accidents should still be expected; the child will indicate readiness for toilet training.
- Throws large ball underhand without losing balance.
- Holds cup or glass (be sure it is unbreakable) in one hand.
- Unbuttons large buttons; unzips large zippers.
- Opens doors by turning doorknobs.
- Grasps large crayon with fist; scribbles enthusiastically on large paper.
- Climbs up on chair, turns around and sits down.
- Enjoys pouring and filling activities—sand, water, Styrofoam peanuts.
- Stacks four to six objects on top of one another.
- Uses feet to propel wheeled riding toys.

Perceptual-Cognitive Development

- Eye–hand movements better coordinated; can put objects together, take them apart; fit large pegs into pegboard.
- Begins to use objects for purposes other than intended (may push a block around as a boat).
- Does simple classification tasks based on one dimension (separates toy dinosaurs from toy cars).
- Stares for long moments; seems fascinated by, or engrossed in, figuring out a situation: where the tennis ball has rolled, where the dog has gone, what has caused a particular noise.
- Attends to self-selected activities for longer periods of time.
- Discovering cause and effect: squeezing the cat makes her scratch.
- Knows where familiar persons should be; notes their absence; finds a hidden object by looking in last hiding place first.
- Names objects in picture books; may pretend to pick something off the page and taste or smell it.
- Recognizes and expresses pain and its location.

Speech and Language Development

- Enjoys being read to if allowed to participate by pointing, making relevant noises, turning pages.
- Realizes that language is effective for getting others to respond to needs and preferences.
- Uses fifty to three hundred different words; vocabulary continuously increasing.

- Has broken the linguistic code; in other words, much of a two-year-old's talk has meaning to him or her.
- Receptive language is more developed than expressive language; most two-year-olds understand significantly more than they can talk about.
- Utters three- and four-word statements; uses conventional word order to form more complete sentences.
- Refers to self as "me" or sometimes "I" rather than by name: "Me go bye-bye"; has no trouble verbalizing "mine."
- Expresses negative statements by tacking on a negative word such as "no" or "not": "Not more milk."
- Repeatedly asks, "What's that?"
- Uses some plurals; tells about objects and events not immediately present (this is both a cognitive and linguistic advance).
- Some stammering and other dysfluencies are common.
- Speech is as much as 65 to 70 percent intelligible.

Personal-Social Development

- Shows signs of empathy and caring: comforts another child who is hurt or frightened; sometimes is overly affectionate in offering hugs and kisses to children.
- Continues to use physical aggression if frustrated or angry (for some children, this is more exaggerated than for others); physical aggression usually lessens as verbal skills improve.
- Temper tantrums likely to peak during this year; cannot be reasoned with while tantrum is in progress.
- Impatient; finds it difficult to wait or take turns.
- Enjoys "helping" with household chores; imitates everyday activities: may try to toilet a stuffed animal, feed a doll.

May demonstrate concern for a hurt friend.

Typically plays alone.

2- YEAR-OLDS

- "Bossy" with parents and caregivers; orders them around, makes demands, expects immediate compliance from adults.
- Watches and imitates the play of other children, but seldom joins in; content to play alone.
- Offers toys to other children, but is usually possessive of playthings; still tends to hoard toys.
- Making choices is difficult; wants it both ways.
- Often defiant; shouting "no" becomes automatic.
- Ritualistic; wants everything "just so"; routines carried out exactly as before; belongings placed "where they belong."

DAILY ROUTINES—TWO-YEAR-OLDS

Eating

- Appetite is fair; fluctuates with periods of growth; lunch is often the preferred meal.
- Sometimes described as a picky or fussy eater; often has strong likes and dislikes (which should be respected); may go on food jags (only eating certain foods, such as peanut butter and jelly sandwiches, macaroni and cheese).
- Likes simple, "recognizable" foods; dislikes mixtures; wants foods served in familiar ways.
- May need between-meal snack; should be of good nutritive value, with "junk" foods unavailable.
- Increasingly able to feed self, but may be "too tired" to do so at times.
- Has good control of cup or glass, though spills happen often.
- Learns table manners by imitating adults and older children.

"Look daddy, all clean!"

Toileting, Bathing, Dressing

- Enjoys bath if allowed ample playtime (*must never be left alone*); may object to being washed; tries to wash self.
- Usually dislikes, even resists, having hair washed.

continued

- Tries to help when being dressed; needs simple, manageable clothing; can usually undress self.
- Shows signs of readiness for bowel training (some children may have already mastered bowel control).
- Stays dry for longer periods of time (one sign of readiness for toilet training); other signs include interest in watching others use toilet, holding a doll or stuffed animal over toilet, clutching self, willingness to sit on potty for a few moments, expressing discomfort about being wet or soiled.

Sleeping

- Amount of nighttime sleep varies (between nine and twelve hours).
- Still requires afternoon nap; needs time to wake up slowly.
- May resist going to bed; usually complies if given ample warning and can depend on familiar bedtime routine (story, talk time, special toy).
- Takes awhile to fall asleep, especially if overly tired; may sing, talk to self, bounce on bed, call for parents, make and remake the bed (again, ways of "winding down").

Play and Social Activity

- Enjoys dressing up and imitating family activities: wearing Father's hat makes a child a "daddy."
- Likes to be around other children, but does not play well with them: observes them intently, imitating their actions (parallel play).
- Displays extreme negativism toward parents and caregivers—an early step toward establishing independence.
- May have an imaginary friend as a constant companion.
- Explores everything in the environment, including other children; may shove or push other children as if to test their reaction.

LEARNING ACTIVITIES

Tips for parents and caregivers:

- Share games, such as large lotto and picture dominoes, that are based on matching colors, animals, facial expressions, and everyday objects.
- Offer manipulative materials to foster problem solving and eye–hand coordina-

DIVERSITY

The composition and character of American society is changing at a pace greater than at anytime in the past. Children attending early childhood programs mirror these societal changes and their growing diversity is representative of currents in the general population. For this reason, it is important to understand the multifaceted quality of diversity and its implications for developmentally appropriate practices.

THE NATURE OF DIVERSITY

Children are each unique in their own way; no two are ever precisely alike. The ongoing and complex interactions that occur between a child's genetic makeup, environments, and accumulation of life experiences are responsible for the differences that distinguish one child from another. It is this 'one-of-a-kindness,' or diversity, that accounts for the individuality of every child and adult.

In the broadest sense, the term diversity is inclusive, referring to a wide range of similarities, as well as differences. Dimensions that are most commonly described include:

- age
- gender
- race and ethnic background
- socio-economic class
- language
- abilities

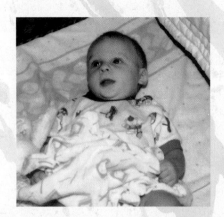

However, diversity issues extend well beyond simple categorization. Family systems, communication styles, religious preferences, education, parenting practices, and community values all play important roles in shaping a child's unique heritage. They also influence a child's sense of identity, or self-concept. Each life experience affects the view children have of themselves. Therefore, efforts must be made to avoid simplistic assumptions and generalizations about aspects of diversity because there are often many variations associated with each dimension. For example, a child who speaks Spanish may come from any number of geographical locations or cultures. Categorizing a child as "Latino" fails to acknowledge individual and cultural differences and, thus, promotes stereotyping.

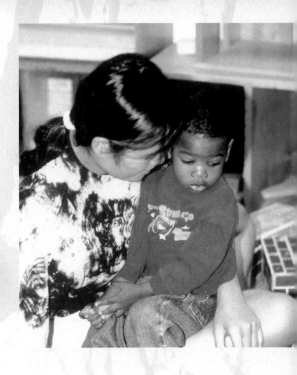

IMPLICATIONS FOR EARLY CHILDHOOD TEACHERS

Teachers clearly occupy key positions of influence with respect to diversity issues. Every phase of planning and implementation within early childhood programs becomes an opportunity for promoting a sense of understanding and acceptance of differences by children and adults. Teachers can help children begin to build a foundation that

 consists of positive attitudes and respect through classroom environments they create, their choices of activities and learning materials, and modeling of sensitive behavior.

VALUES AND ATTITUDES

It is always important for teachers to examine their own attitudes and beliefs about various cultures, practices, religions, abilities, and limitations in order to recognize potential biases. Personal ignorance and prejudice limit a teacher's effectiveness in promoting acceptance and celebration of individual differences in the classroom. This self-examination process also opens doors to opportunities for acquiring new information and improved understanding.

Early childhood settings present many valuable opportunities for helping children gain positive attitudes toward others. A value-neutral classroom environment encourages children to express their questions and curiosities about individual differences.

Answers given in a direct and objective manner promote an atmosphere of acceptance and respect. Activities that are integrated into daily learning experiences, rather than taught as separate and occasional lessons, help children develop a greater appreciation for diversity. Over time, children will learn to treat one another with respect, fairness, and friendship and to value the unique contributions of each individual.

COMMUNICATION

Quality early childhood programs are based on effective communication in a context that supports an appreciation of diversity. Teachers should encourage all children to communicate in whatever form their abilities allow. Teachers acknowledge and show respect for cultural variations in children's language, and provide learning experiences that value these differences.

Misunderstandings can be prevented when time is taken to learn the significance and variations of communication styles, including nonverbal behaviors such as facial expressions, eye contact, touch, and posture. Knowing, for example, that direct eye contact is considered disrespectful among some cultures and, therefore, is purposefully avoided, reduces the chance of misinterpreting this behavior as inattention, indifference, or rudeness.

Children's communication needs can be met through daily classroom experiences that embrace the richness of cultural differences. Activities, especially those involving art, music, storytelling, and dramatic play, facilitate children's mastery of basic communication skills. They are also effective for improving language proficiency, learning to ask questions, exploring differences, expressing opinions freely and, thus, broadening a child's social competency.

LEARNING EXPERIENCES

Educational programs that value diversity provide experiences that broaden children's understanding of other cultures and abilities. They also accommodate children's differences in interests and learning styles. Teachers recognize that children's personalities, skills, talents, language, and cultural backgrounds all influence the context in which they learn. Teachers know their children and select educational practices and instructional materials that are meaningful and relevant to the diverse nature of children. Teachers view families as valuable resources and encourage them to participate in their children's learning experiences. Every effort is made to avoid materials and practices that are disrespectful or support biased information.

ASSESSMENT

Evaluation of children's abilities and developmental progress also respects their diversity. Teachers choose assessment tools and practices that take into account differences in children's backgrounds, cultural expectations, learning styles, and physical, mental, and language limitations. They identify evaluation measures that acknowledge children's strengths, as well as their weaknesses. Observations of children in their natural settings are included so as to be sensitive to  matters of diversity and to avoid tendencies for biased assumptions. Evaluation also includes the family, and takes their expectations into consideration when establishing realistic goals and objectives for children. Teachers who value diversity also recognize when circumstances make assessment inappropriate or invalid.

WORKING WITH FAMILIES

Programs that value diversity involve
families in children's learning experiences. Family members are invited to
share their traditions, language,
celebrations, foods, music,
stories, and special talents.
They are welcomed at
every opportunity - their
presence and participation
is encouraged and valued.
Communication between
families and teachers is
frequent, supportive,
respectful, and builds
important partnerships.

Family involvement brings an un-
paralleled richness to early childhood
programs, and enhances children's
understanding and acceptance of
individual differences. It also helps
children develop a stronger sense of
self-identity and self-worth. Similarly,
families benefit from involvement in
their children's education. Improved
understanding and consistency result
when ties are strengthened between
children's homes and school.

The challenge clearly remains - to
continue working toward greater
understanding, sensitivity, and acceptance of individual differences.

tion: large beads for stringing, brightly colored cubes, puzzle boxes, large, plastic interlocking bricks.

- Provide toy replicas of farm and zoo animals, families, cars, trucks, and planes for sorting and imaginative play.
- Read to the child regularly; provide colorful picture books for naming objects and describing everyday events; use simple illustrated storybooks (one line per page) so the child can learn to tell the story.
- Share nursery rhymes, simple finger plays, and action songs; respond to, imitate, and make up simple games based on the child's spontaneous rhyming or chanting.
- Set out (and keep a close eye on) washable paints, markers, chalk, large crayons, and large paper for artistic expression.
- Help with make-believe activities; for example: save empty cereal boxes, discarded cans with intact labels for playing store.
- Provide wagons; large trucks and cars that can be loaded, pushed, or sat on; doll carriage or stroller; a rocking boat; bean bags and rings for tossing.

DEVELOPMENTAL ALERTS

Check with a health care provider or early childhood specialist if, by the third birthday, the child *does not*:

- Eat a fairly well-rounded diet, even though amounts are limited.
- Walk confidently with few stumbles or falls; climb steps with help.
- Avoid bumping into objects.
- Carry out simple two-step directions: "Come to Daddy and bring your book;" express desires; ask questions.
- Point to and name familiar objects; use two- or three-word sentences.
- Enjoy being read to.
- Show interest in playing with other children: watching, perhaps imitating.
- Indicate a beginning interest in toilet training.
- Sort familiar objects according to a single characteristic, such as type, color, or size.

2-YEAR-OLDS

Test Your Knowledge

REVIEW QUESTIONS

1. Identify two motor skills that one- and two-year-olds typically acquire.

   a. one-year-old:

      1.

      2.

   b. two-year-old:

      1.

      2.

2. List three developmentally appropriate activities for a two-year-old (based on perceptual-cognitive and motor skills).

   a.

   b.

   c.

3. List three ways in which a one-year-old may begin to assert independence.

   a.

   b.

   c.

TRUE OR FALSE

1. A two-year-old can be expected to follow three-step instructions.

2. The ideal way to stop a temper tantrum is to pick the child up, set the child in a chair, and discuss the problem.

3. Parents should be concerned about a toddler who "doesn't seem to eat much."

4. Most two-year-olds have given up afternoon naps.

5. Toddlers should be punished for constantly getting into things.

6. Most two-year-olds can use language to make requests.

7. Children exhibit certain recognizable behaviors when they are ready to begin toilet training.

8. Height and weight increase rapidly during this period.

MULTIPLE CHOICE   *Select one or more correct answers from the lists below.*

1. It is reasonable to expect most one-year-olds to
   a. use a spoon with full control.
   b. take off own shoes and stockings.
   c. catch a small ball.

2. Two-year-olds are most likely to engage in the type of play that is referred to as:
   a. solitary.
   b. parallel.
   c. cooperative.

3. Caregivers should be concerned about the language development of a two-year-old who consistently utters statements such as
   a. "No want mittens on."
   b. "Me go."
   c. "Shoes on right feets?"

4. Bedtime can be made easier by
   a. letting the child decide when and how bedtime should proceed.
   b. following the same basic routine every night.
   c. planning thirty minutes of vigorous activity before bedtime to make the child physically tired.

5. Changes in perceptual-cognitive development that occur include the ability to
   a. take apart a stacking toy and put it back together.
   b. pull to a standing position.
   c. separate blocks into piles of red, yellow, blue.

CHAPTER 6

THE PRESCHOOLER

Typically, three-, four-, and five-year-olds are full of energy, eagerness, and curiosity. They seem to be constantly on the move as they engross themselves totally in whatever captures their interest at the moment. During these years, motor skills are being perfected. Creativity and imagination come into everything, from dramatic play to artwork to storytelling. Vocabulary and intellectual skills expand rapidly, allowing the child to express ideas, solve problems, and plan ahead. Preschool children strongly believe in their own opinions. At the same time, they are developing some sense of the needs of others and some degree of control over their own behavior. They strive for independence, yet they need reassurance that an adult is available to give assistance, to comfort, or to rescue, if need be.

THE THREE-YEAR-OLD

DEVELOPMENTAL PROFILES AND GROWTH PATTERNS

Three-year-olds tend to be more peaceful, relaxed, and cooperative. Conflicts with adults, growing out of the two-year-old's struggle for independence, are fewer and less intense. In fact, many three-year-olds are willing to abide by parents' and caregivers' directions much of the time. They are able to delay their own gratification longer; that is, they have less need to have what they want "right now." They take obvious delight in themselves and life in general and show an irrepressible urge to find out all about everything in the world around them.

Growth and Physical Development

- Growth is steady though slower than in the first two years.
- Height increases 2 to 3 inches (5–7.6 cm) per year; average height is 38 to 40 inches (96.5–101.6 cm), nearly double the child's birth length.

Appearance becomes more adult-like.

- Adult height can be predicted from measurements of height at three years of age; males are approximately 53 percent of their adult height and females, 57 percent.
- Weight gains average 3 to 5 pounds (1.4–2.3 kg) per year; weight averages 30 to 38 pounds (13.6–17.2 kg).
- Heart rate (pulse) averages 90 to 110 beats per minute.
- Respiratory rate is twenty to thirty, depending on activity level; child continues to breathe abdominally.

**Walks up and down stairs using
alternating feet.**

- Temperature averages 96° to 99.4°F (35.5–37.4°C); is affected by exertion, illness, and stress.
- Growth of legs is more rapid than growth of arms, giving the three-year-old a taller, thinner, adult-like appearance.
- Circumference of head and chest is equal; head size is in better proportion to the body.
- Neck appears to lengthen as "baby fat" disappears.
- Posture is more erect; abdomen no longer protrudes.
- Still appears slightly knock-kneed.
- Has a full set of "baby" teeth.
- Needs to consume approximately 1,500 calories daily.
- Visual acuity is approximately 20/40 using the Snellen E chart.

Motor Development

- Walks up and down stairs unassisted, using alternating feet; may jump from bottom step, landing on both feet.
- Can balance momentarily on one foot.
- Kicks a large ball.
- Feeds self; needs minimal assistance.
- Jumps in place.
- Pedals a small tricycle or Bigwheel.
- Throws a ball overhand; aim and distance are limited.
- Catches a large bounced ball with both arms extended.
- Enjoys swinging on a swing (not too high or too fast).

Enjoys swinging.

- Shows improved control of crayons or makers; uses vertical, horizontal and circular strokes.
- Holds crayon or marker between first two fingers and thumb (tripod grasp), not in a fist as earlier.
- Can turn pages of a book one at a time.
- Enjoys building with blocks.
- Builds a tower of eight or more blocks.
- Enjoys playing with clay; pounds, rolls, and squeezes it.
- May begin to show **hand dominance.**
- Carries a container of liquid, such as a cup of milk or bowl of water, without much spilling; pours liquid from pitcher into another container.
- Manipulates large buttons and zippers on clothing.
- Washes and dries hands; brushes own teeth, but not thoroughly.
- Usually achieves complete bladder control during this time.

Perceptual and Cognitive Development

- Listens attentively to age-appropriate stories.
- Makes relevant comments during stories, especially those that relate to home and family events.
- Likes to look at books and may pretend to "read" to others or explain pictures.
- Enjoys stories with riddles, guessing, and "suspense."

Holds marker in tripod grasp.

Builds tower of eight or more blocks.

hand dominance—*Preference for using one hand over the other; most individuals are said to be either right- or left-handed.*

May "read" to others or explain pictures.

- Points with a fair degree of accuracy to correct pictures when given sound-alike words: *keys-cheese; fish-dish; mouse-mouth.*
- Plays realistically:
    —Feeds doll, puts down for nap, covers it.
    —Hooks truck and trailer together, loads truck, drives away making motor noises.
- Places eight to ten pegs in pegboard, or six round and six square blocks in formboard.
- Attempts to draw; imperfectly copies circles, squares, and some letters.
- Understands triangle, circle, square; can point to requested shape.
- Sorts objects logically on the basis of one dimension, such as color, shape, or size; usually chooses color or size as basis for classification.

Attempts to reproduce shapes.

Imitates models of "trains" and "bridges."

- Shows understanding of basic size-shape comparisons much of the time; will indicate which is bigger when shown a tennis ball and a golf ball; also understands smaller of the two.
- Names and matches, at a minimum, primary colors: red, yellow, blue.
- Arranges cubes in horizontal line; also positions cubes to form a bridge.
- Counts objects out loud.
- Points to picture that has "more": cars, planes, or kittens.
- Shows some understanding of duration of time by using phrases such as "all the time," "all day," "for two days"; some confusion remains: "I didn't take a nap tomorrow."

Speech and Language Development

- Talks about objects, events, and people not present: "Jerry has a pool in his yard."
- Talks about the actions of others: "Daddy's mowing the grass."
- Adds information to what has just been said: "Yeah, and then he grabbed it back."
- Answers simple questions appropriately.
- Asks increasing numbers of questions, particularly about location and identity of objects and people.
- Uses an increasing number of speech forms that keep conversation going: "What did he do next?" "How come she hid?"
- Calls attention to self, objects, or events in the environment: "Watch my helicopter fly."
- Promotes the behavior of others: "Let's jump in the water. You go first."
- Joins in social interaction rituals: "Hi," "Bye," "Please."
- Comments about objects and ongoing events: "There's a house"; "The tractor's pushing a boat."
- Vocabulary has increased; now uses three hundred to one thousand words.
- Recites nursery rhymes, sings songs.

Counts out loud: 1, 2, 3, 4. . . .

Answers questions about familiar objects and events.

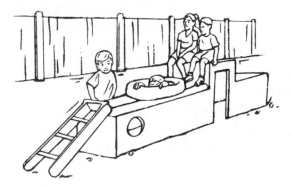

Engages in make-believe.

- Speech is understandable most of the time.
- Produces expanded noun phrases: "big, brown dog."
- Produces verbs with "ing" endings; uses "-s" to indicate more than one; often puts "-s" on already pluralized forms: geeses, mices.
- Indicates negatives by inserting "no" or "not" before a simple noun or verb phrase: "Not baby."
- Answers "What are you doing?", "What is this?", and "Where?" questions dealing with familiar objects and events.

Personal-Social Development

- Seems to understand taking turns, but not always willing to do so.
- Friendly; laughs frequently; is eager to please.
- Has occasional nightmares and fears the dark, monsters, or fire.
- Joins in simple games and group activities, sometimes hesitantly.
- Often talks to self.
- Uses objects symbolically in play: block of wood may be a truck, a ramp, a bat.
- Observes other children playing; may join in for a short time; often plays parallel to other children.
- Defends toys and possessions; may become aggressive at times by grabbing a toy, hitting another child, hiding toys.
- Engages in make-believe play alone and with other children.
- Shows affection toward children who are younger or children who get hurt.
- Sits and listens to stories up to ten minutes at a time; does not bother other children listening to story and resents being bothered.
- May continue to have a special blanket, stuffed animal, or toy for comfort.

DAILY ROUTINES—THREE-YEAR-OLDS

Eating

- Appetite fair; prefers small servings. Dislikes many cooked vegetables; eats almost everything else; should never be forced to eat.
- Feeds self independently if hungry. Uses spoon in semi-adult fashion; may spear with fork.
- Dawdles over food, or plays with it, when not hungry.
- Can pour milk and juice with fewer spills; can serve individual portions from a serving dish with some prompts ("Fill it up to the line"; "Take only two spoonsful").
- Drinks a great deal of milk. (Be sure child does not fill up on milk to the exclusion of other needed foods.)

Toileting, Bathing, Dressing

- Does a fair job of washing self in bathtub; often resists getting out of tub.
- Takes care of own toilet needs during the daytime (boys, especially, may continue to have wet-pants days).
- Some sleep through the night without wetting the bed; others are in transition—they may stay dry at night for days or weeks, then go back to night-wetting for a period.
- Better at undressing than dressing, though capable of putting on some articles of clothing.
- More adept at managing large buttons, snaps, and zippers.

Sleeping

- Usually sleeps ten to twelve hours at night, waking up about 7 or 8 A.M.; some children are awake much earlier.
- May no longer take an afternoon nap; continues to benefit from a midday quiet time.
- Can get self ready for bed. Has given up many earlier bedtime rituals; still needs a bedtime story or song and tucking-in.
- May have dreams that cause the child to awaken.
- May wander at night; quiet firmness may be needed in returning child to own bed.

continued

Play and Social Activity

- The "me too" age; wants to be included in everything.
- Spontaneous group play for short periods; very social; beginning to play cooperatively.
- May argue or quarrel with other children; adults should allow children to settle their own disagreements unless physical harm is threatened.
- Loves dress-up, dramatic play that involves everyday work activities. Strong gender and role stereotypes: "Boys can't be nurses."
- Responds well to options rather than commands: "Do you want to put your pajamas on before or after the story?"
- Sharing still difficult, but seems to understand the concept.

LEARNING ACTIVITIES

Tips for parents and caregivers:

- Allow the child to create new uses for everyday household items and discards: blanket over a table to make a cave; utensils for pretend cooking; discarded mail for playing mail carrier; hose with trickle of water for washing tricycle or wagon; oil can for servicing the vehicles.
- Provide somewhat more complex manipulative materials: parquetry blocks; pegboards with multicolored pegs; various items to count, sort, and match; construction sets with medium-size, interlocking pieces.
- Offer art and craft materials that encourage experimentation: crayons, washable markers, chalk, modeling clay, round-tipped scissors, papers, glue, paints, and large brushes (supervision required).
- Keep on hand a plentiful supply of books about animals, families, everyday events, alphabet and counting activities, poems and rhymes; continue daily reading sessions.
- Make regular trips to the library; allow plenty of time for child to make own book selections.
- Provide three-wheeled tricycle or similar riding toys that build eye–hand–foot dexterity through steering and maneuvering; also wheelbarrow and garden tools, doll stroller, shopping cart.
- Go for walks with the child, *at the child's pace;* allow ample time for child to explore, observe, and collect rocks, leaves, seed pods; name and talk about things along the way.

DEVELOPMENTAL ALERTS

Check with a health care provider or early childhood specialist if, by the fourth birthday, the child *does not:*

- Have intelligible speech most of the time.
- Understand and follow simple commands and directions.
- State own name and age.
- Enjoy playing near or with other children.
- Use three- to four-word sentences.
- Ask questions.
- Stay with an activity for three or four minutes; play alone several minutes at a time.
- Jump in place without falling.
- Balance on one foot, at least briefly.
- Help with dressing self.

THE FOUR-YEAR-OLD

Tireless bundles of energy, brimful of ideas, overflowing with chatter and activity—these are the characteristics typical of most four-year-olds. Bouts of stubbornness and arguments between child and parent or caregiver may be frequent. Children test limits, practice self-confidence and firm up a growing need for independence; many are loud, boisterous, even belligerent. They try adults' patients with silly talk and silly jokes, constant chatter and endless questions. At the same time, they have many lovable qualities. They are enthusiastic, try hard to be helpful, have lively imaginations, and can plan ahead to some extent: "When we get home, I'll make you a picture."

DEVELOPMENTAL PROFILES AND GROWTH PATTERNS

Growth and Physical Characteristics

- Gains approximately 4 to 5 pounds (1.8–2.3 kg) per year; weighs an average of 32 to 40 pounds (14.5–18.2 kg).
- Grows 2 to 2.5 inches (5.0–6.4 cm) in height per year; is approximately 40 to 45 inches (101.6–114 cm) tall.
- Heart rate (pulse) averages 90 to 110 beats per minute.

Affectionate toward younger children.

- Respiratory rate ranges from twenty to thirty, varying with activity and emotional state.
- Body temperature ranges from 98 to 99.4°F (36.6–37.4°C).
- Head circumference is usually not measured after age three.
- Requires approximately 1,700 calories daily.
- Hearing acuity can be assessed by child's correct usage of sounds and language; also, by the child's appropriate responses to questions and instructions.
- Visual acuity is 20/30 as measured on the Snellen E chart.

Motor Development

- Walks a straight line (tape or chalkline on the floor).
- Hops on one foot.
- Pedals and steers a wheeled toy with confidence; turns corners, avoids obstacles and oncoming "traffic."
- Climbs ladders, trees, playground equipment.
- Jumps over objects 5 or 6 inches high; lands with both feet together.
- Runs, starts, stops, and moves around obstacles with ease.
- Throws a ball overhand; distance and aim improving.
- Builds a tower with ten or more blocks.
- Forms shapes and objects out of clay: cookies, snakes, simple animals.
- Reproduces some shapes and letters.
- Holds a crayon or marker using a tripod grasp.
- Paints and draws with purpose; may have an idea in mind, but often has trouble implementing it so calls the creation something else.
- Becomes more accurate at hitting nails and pegs with hammer.
- Threads small wooden beads on a string.

Walks a straight line.

Perceptual-Cognitive Development

- Stacks at least five graduated cubes from largest to smallest; builds a pyramid of six blocks.
- Indicates if paired words sound the same or different: *sheet/feet, ball/wall.*
- Near the end of this year, may name eighteen to twenty uppercase letters and write several; print own name; recognize some printed words (especially those that have a special meaning for the child).

Reproduces shapes and letters.

Answers questions about "how many."

- A few children are beginning to read simple books, such as alphabet books with only a few words per page and many pictures.
- Likes stories about how things grow and how things operate.
- Delights in wordplay, creating silly language.
- Understands the concepts of "tallest," "biggest," "same," and "more"; selects the picture that has the "most houses" or the "biggest dogs."
- Rote counts to 20 or more.
- Understands the sequence of daily events: "When we get up in the morning, we get dressed, have breakfast, brush our teeth, and go to school."
- When looking at pictures, can recognize and identify missing puzzle parts (of person, car, animal).

Speech and Language Development

- Uses the prepositions "on," "in," and "under."
- Uses possessives consistently: "hers," "theirs," "baby's."
- Answers "Whose?", "Who?", "Why?", and "How many?"
- Produces elaborate sentence structures: "The cat ran under the house before I could see what color it was."
- Speech is almost entirely intelligible.
- Begins to correctly use the past tense of verbs: "Mommy closed the door," "Daddy went to work."
- Refers to activities, events, objects, and people that are not present.
- Changes tone of voice and sentence structure to adapt to listener's level of understanding: To baby brother, "Milk gone?" To Mother, "Did the baby drink all of his milk?"
- States first and last name, gender, siblings' names, and sometimes own telephone number.
- Answers appropriately when asked what to do if tired, cold, or hungry.

- Recites and sings simple songs and rhymes.

Personal-Social Development

- Outgoing; friendly; overly enthusiastic at times.
- Moods change rapidly and unpredictably; laughing one minute, crying the next; may throw tantrum over minor frustrations (a block structure that will not balance); sulk over being left out.
- Imaginary playmates or companions are common; holds conversations and shares strong emotions with this invisible friend.
- Boasts, exaggerates, and "bends" the truth with made-up stories or claims of boldness; tests the limits with "bathroom" talk.
- Cooperates with others; participates in group activities.
- Shows pride in accomplishments; seeks frequent adult approval.
- Often appears selfish; not always able to take turns or to understand taking turns under some conditions; tattles on other children.
- Insists on trying to do things independently, but may get so frustrated as to verge on tantrums when problems arise: paint that drips, paper airplane that will not fold right.
- Enjoys role-playing and make-believe activities.
- Relies (most of the time) on verbal rather than physical aggression; may yell angrily rather than hit to make a point; threatens: "You can't come to my birthday party."
- Name-calling and taunting are often used as ways of excluding other children.
- Establishes close relationships with playmates; beginning to have "best" friends.

Plays cooperatively with others.

Takes pride in accomplishments.

DAILY ROUTINES—FOUR-YEAR-OLDS

Eating

- Appetite fluctuates from very good to fair.
- May develop dislikes of certain foods and refuse them to the point of tears if pushed (such pressure can cause serious adult–child conflict).
- Uses all eating utensils; quite skilled at spreading jelly or peanut butter or cutting soft foods such as bread.
- Eating and talking get in each other's way; talking usually takes precedence over eating.
- Likes to help in the preparation of a meal; dumping premeasured ingredients, washing vegetables, setting the table.

Toileting, Bathing, Dressing

- Takes care of own toileting needs; often demands privacy in the bathroom.
- Does an acceptable job of bathing and brushing teeth, but should receive assistance (or subtle inspection) from adults regularly.
- Dresses self; can lace shoes, button buttons, buckle belts. Gets frustrated if problems arise in getting dressed while stubbornly refusing much-needed adult help.
- Can sort and fold own clean clothes, put clothes away, hang up towels, straighten room; easily distracted, however.

Sleeping

- Averages ten to twelve hours of sleep at night; may still take an afternoon nap.
- Bedtime usually not a problem if cues, rather than orders, signal the time: when the story is finished, when the clock hands are in a certain position.
- Some children fear the dark, but usually a light left on in the hall is all that is needed.
- Getting up to use the toilet may require helping the child settle down for sleep again.

Play and Social Activities

- Playmates are important; plays cooperatively some of the time; may be "bossy."

continued

- Takes turns; shares (most of the time); wants to be with children every waking moment.
- Needs (and seeks out) adult approval and attention; may comment, "Look what I did."
- Understands and needs limits (but not too constraining); will abide by rules most of the time.
- Brags about possessions; shows off; boasts about family members.

LEARNING ACTIVITIES

Tips for parents and caregivers:

- Join in simple board and card games (picture lotto, Candyland) that depend on chance, not strategy; emphasis should be on playing, not winning. (Learning to be a "good sport" does not come until much later.)
- Provide puzzles with five to ten pieces (number depends on the child), counting and alphabet games, matching games, such as more detailed lotto.
- Offer various kinds of simple scientific and math materials: ruler, compass, magnifying glass, simple scales; activities, such as collecting leaves, growing worms, sprouting seeds.
- Appreciate (and sometimes join in) the child's spontaneous rhyming, chanting, silly name-calling, jokes, riddles.
- Continue daily read-aloud times; encourage the child to supply words or phrases, to guess *what comes next,* to retell the story (or parts of it); introduce the idea of "looking things up" in a simple picture dictionary or encyclopedia; go to the library regularly, allowing the child ample time to choose books.
- Encourage all kinds of vigorous outdoor activity; water play in sprinkler or plastic pool (*pool requires adult presence*); offer unpressured swimming, tumbling, or dancing lessons.

DEVELOPMENTAL ALERTS

Check with a health care provider or early childhood specialist if, by the fifth birthday, the child *does not:*

- State own name in full.
- Recognize simple shapes: circle, square, triangle.
- Catch a large ball when bounced.
- Speak so as to be understood by strangers.
- Have good control of posture and movement.
- Hop on one foot.
- Appear interested in, and responsive to, surroundings.
- Respond to statements without constantly asking to have them repeated.
- Dress self with minimal adult assistance; manage buttons, zippers.
- Take care of own toilet needs; have good bowel and bladder control with infrequent accidents.

THE FIVE-YEAR-OLD

More in control of themselves, both physically and emotionally, most five-year-olds appear to be in a period of relative calm. The child is friendly and outgoing much of the time and is becoming self-confident and reliable. The world is expanding beyond home and family and child-care center. Friendships and group activities are of major importance.

Constant practice and mastery of skills in all areas of development is the major focus of the five-year-old. However, this quest for mastery, coupled with a high energy level and robust self-confidence, can lead to mishap. Eagerness to do and explore often interferes with the ability to foresee danger or potentially disastrous consequences. Therefore, the child's safety and the prevention of accidents must be a major concern of parents and caregivers. At the same time, adults' concerns must be handled in ways that do not interfere with the child's sense of competence and self-esteem.

May begin to lose teeth.

DEVELOPMENTAL PROFILES AND GROWTH PATTERNS

Growth and Physical Characteristics

- Gains 4 to 5 pounds (1.8–2.3 kg) per year; weighs an average of 38 to 45 pounds (17.3–20.5 kg).
- Grows an average of 2 to 2.5 inches (5.1–6.4 cm) per year; is approximately 42 to 46 inches (106.7–116.8 cm) tall.
- Heart rate (pulse) is approximately 90 to 110 beats per minute.
- Respiratory rate ranges from twenty to thirty, depending on activity and emotional status.
- Body temperature is stabilized at 98° to 99.4°F.
- Head size is approximately that of an adult's.
- May begin to lose "baby" (deciduous) teeth.
- Body is adult-like in proportion.
- Requires approximately 1,800 calories daily.
- Visual acuity is 20/20 using the Snellen E chart.
- Visual tracking and **binocular vision** are well developed.

Motor Development

- Walks backwards, heel to toe.
- Walks unassisted up and down stairs, alternating feet.

Balances on either foot.

Builds structures from models.

---

binocular vision—*Both eyes working together, sending a single image to the brain.*

- May learn to turn somersaults (should be taught the right way in order to avoid injury).
- Can touch toes without flexing knees.
- Walks a balance beam.
- Learns to skip using alternative feet.
- Catches a ball thrown from 3 feet away.
- Rides a tricycle or wheeled toy with speed and skillful steering; some children learning to ride bicycles, usually with training wheels.
- Jumps or hops forward ten times in a row without falling.
- Balances on either foot with good control for ten seconds.
- Builds three-dimensional structures with small cubes by copying from a picture or model.
- Reproduces many shapes and letters: square, triangle, *A, I, O, U, C, H, L, T.*
- Demonstrates fair control of pencil or marker; may begin to color within the lines.
- Cuts on the line with scissors (not perfectly).
- Hand dominance is fairly well established.

Perceptual and Cognitive Development

- Forms rectangle from two triangular cuts.
- Builds steps with set of small blocks.
- Understands concept of *same* shape, *same* size.
- Sorts objects on the basis of two dimensions, such as color and form.
- Sorts a variety of objects so that all things in the group have a single common feature (classification skill: all are food items or boats or animals).
- Understands the concepts of smallest and shortest; places objects in order from shortest to tallest, smallest to largest.

Cuts on the line but not perfectly.

Identifies and names at least four colors.

Participates in elaborate make-believe.

- Identifies objects with specified serial position: first, second, last.
- Rote counts to 20 and above; many children count to 100.
- Recognizes numerals from 1 to 10.
- Understands the concepts of less than: "Which bowl has less water?"
- Understands the terms *dark, light,* and *early:* "I got up early, before anyone else. It was still dark."
- Relates clock time to daily schedule: "Time to turn on TV when the little hand points to 5."
- Some children can tell time on the hour: five o'clock, two o'clock.
- Knows what a calendar is for.
- Recognizes and identifies penny, nickel, and dime; beginning to count and save money.
- Many children know alphabet and names of upper- and lowercase letters.
- Understands the concept of half; can say how many pieces an object has when it's been cut in half.
- Asks innumerable questions: Why? What? Where? When?
- Eager to learn new things.

Speech and Language Development

- Vocabulary of 1,500 words or more.
- Tells a familiar story while looking at pictures in a book.
- Defines simple words by function: a ball is to bounce; a bed is to sleep in.

- Identifies and names four to eight colors.
- Recognizes the humor in simple jokes; makes up jokes and riddles.
- Produces sentences with five to seven words; much longer sentences are not unusual.
- States the name of own city or town, birthday, and parents' names.
- Answers telephone appropriately; calls person to phone or takes a brief message.
- Speech is almost entirely intelligible.
- Uses "would" and "could" appropriately.
- Uses past tense of irregular verbs consistently: "went," "caught," "swam."
- Uses past-tense inflection (-ed) appropriately to mark regular verbs: "jumped," "rained," "washed."

Personal-Social Development

- Enjoys friendships; often has one or two special playmates.
- Is often generous: shares toys, takes turns, plays cooperatively (with occasional lapses).
- Participates in group play and shared activities with other children; suggests imaginative and elaborate play ideas.
- Is affectionate and caring, especially toward younger or injured children and animals.
- Generally does what parent or caregiver requests; follows directions and carries out responsibilities most of the time.
- Continues to need adult comfort and reassurance, but may be less open in seeking and accepting comfort.
- Has better self-control; fewer dramatic swings of emotions.
- Likes to tell jokes, entertain, and make people laugh.
- Boastful about accomplishments.

DAILY ROUTINES—FIVE-YEAR-OLDS

Eating

- Eats well, but not at every meal.
- Likes familiar foods; prefers most vegetables raw.
- Often adopts food dislikes of family members and caregivers.
- "Makes" breakfast (pours cereal, gets out milk and juice) and lunch (spreads peanut butter and jam on bread).

continued

Toileting, Bathing, Dressing

- Takes full responsibility for own toileting; may put off going to the bathroom until an accident occurs or is barely avoided.
- Bathes fairly independently, but needs some help getting started.
- Dresses self completely; learning to tie shoes, sometimes aware when clothing is on wrong side out or backwards.
- Careless with clothes; leaves them strewn about; needs many reminders to pick them up.
- Uses tissue for blowing nose, but often does a careless or incomplete job; forgets to throw tissue away.

Sleeping

- Independently manages all routines associated with getting ready for bed; can help with younger brother's or sister's bedtime routine.
- Averages ten or eleven hours of sleep per night. The five-year-old may still nap.
- Dreams and nightmares are common.
- Going to sleep is often delayed if the day has been especially exciting or if long anticipated events are scheduled for the next day.

Play and Social Activities

- Helpful and cooperative in carrying out family chores and routines.
- Somewhat rigid about the "right" way to do something and the "right" answers to questions.
- Fearful that mother may not come back; very attached to home and family; willing to have an adventure to some degree, but wants the adventure to begin and end at home.
- Plays well with other children, but three may be a crowd: two five-year-olds will often exclude the third.
- Shows affection and protection toward younger sister or brother; may feel overburdened at times if younger child demands too much attention.

5-YEAR-OLDS

LEARNING ACTIVITIES

Tips for parents and caregivers:

- Provide inexpensive materials (computer paper, wallpaper books, paint samples, scraps of fabric) for cutting, pasting, painting, coloring, folding; offer such things as simple looms for weaving, simple sewing activities, smaller beads for string-ing; wood scraps and tools for simple carpentry.

- Continue to collect props and dress-up clothes that allow more detailed acting out of family and worker roles; visit and talk about community activities—house building, post office and mail pickups, farmers' market; encourage play with puppets; assist in creating a stage (a cut-out carton works well).
- Use a variety of books to help the child learn about the many joys and functions of books in everyday life; continue to read aloud, regularly and frequently.
- Encourage the growing interest in paper-and-pencil games and number-, letter-, and word-recognition games that the child often invents, but may need adult help in carrying out.
- Plan cooking experiences that allow the child to chop vegetables, roll out cookies, measure, mix, and stir.
- Help set up improvised target games that promote eye–hand coordination: bean bag toss, bowling, ring toss, low hoop and basketball; ensure opportunities for vigorous play: wheel toys; jungle gyms and parallel bars; digging, raking, and hauling.

DEVELOPMENTAL ALERTS

Check with a health care provider or early childhood specialist if, by the sixth birthday, the child *does not*:

- Alternate feet when walking up and down stairs.
- Speak in a moderate voice; neither too loud, too soft, too high, too low.
- Follow simple directions in stated order: "Please go to the cupboard, get a cup, and bring it to me.
- Use four to five words in acceptable sentence structure.
- Cut on a line with scissors.
- Sit still and listen to an entire short story (five to seven minutes).
- Maintain eye contact when spoken to (unless this is a cultural taboo).
- Play well with other children.
- Perform most self-grooming tasks independently: brush teeth, wash hands and face.

Test Your Knowledge

REVIEW QUESTIONS

1. List three motor skills that appear between two and five years of age.

   a.

   b.

   c.

2. List a social-personal skill typical of each of the following ages.

   a. three-year-olds:

   b. four-year-olds:

   c. five-year-olds:

3. List three major speech and language skills, in order of their developmental appearance, between three and five years of age.

   a.

   b.

   c.

TRUE OR FALSE

1. Growth is slow and steady during most of the preschool years.
2. A full set of baby teeth is usually in place by three or four years of age.
3. Typically, bladder control is achieved between three and five years of age.
4. Fifteen to eighteen hours of sleep at night is characteristic of the older preschool-age child.
5. Silly talk and silly jokes (that is, silly to adults) seem to go hand in hand with the development of language skills in the preschool-age child.
6. Imaginary playmates are common among preschoolers.
7. Fluctuations in appetite are normal during the preschool years.
8. Safety and prevention of accidents need not concern adults because preschool-age children have learned to be cautious.

9. It is most unusual for five-year-olds to have dreams or nightmares.

10. Defining nouns by function (what the object does) is characteristic of the older preschool-age child: "A kite is to fly," "A book is to read."

MULTIPLE CHOICE   *Select one or more correct answers from the list below.*

1. Which of the following might be cause for concern if a three-year-old is not doing it?

    a. talking clearly enough to be understood most of the time.

    b. stating own name.

    c. using scissors to cut out shapes accurately.

2. Which of the following might be of concern if a four-year-old is not doing it?

    a. hopping on one foot.

    b. printing all letters of the alphabet legibly and in order.

    c. dressing self with only occasional help from the parent or caregiver.

3. Which of the following might be cause for concern if a child is not doing it by age five?

    a. listening to a story for five minutes.

    b. making an acceptable sentence using four or five words.

    c. alternating feet when walking down the stairs.

4. Which of the following describes most healthy preschool-age children?

    a. eager to find out all about everything they contact.

    b. vocabulary and intellectual skills expanding rapidly.

    c. content to stay close to adults; not willing to begin to branch out into activities with other children.

5. Which of the following expectations of preschool-age children are unrealistic?

    a. explaining why they did something unacceptable.

    b. being responsible for the care and safety of younger brothers and sisters.

    c. answering the telephone pleasantly.

CHAPTER 7

THE PRIMARY SCHOOL CHILD

SIX-, SEVEN-, AND EIGHT-YEAR-OLDS

The period following the preschool years is especially remarkable. Children are in a stage of developmental integration, organizing and combining various developmental skills to accomplish increasingly complex tasks. At this age, boys and girls alike are becoming competent at taking care of their own personal needs—washing, dressing, toileting, eating, getting up, and getting ready for school. They observe family rules

Understands family rules about television viewing.

about mealtimes, television, and needs for privacy. They can be trusted to run errands and carry out simple responsibilities at home and school. In other words, these children are in control of themselves and their immediate world. Above all, six-, seven-, and eight-year-olds are ready and eager to go to school, even though somewhat apprehensive when the time actually arrives. Going to school creates anxieties, such as arriving on time, remembering to bring back assigned items, and walking home alone or to after-school child care.

Learning to read is the most complex perceptual task the child encounters following the preschool years. It involves recognizing the visual letter symbols and associating them with their spoken sound. It also means that children must learn to combine letters to form words, and to put these words together to form intelligible thoughts that can be read or spoken. Complex as the task is, most children between six and eight years of age become so adept at reading that the skill is soon taken for granted.

Sensory activities are essential to all learning in young children. Developmental kindergartens and primary classes recognize this. They emphasize sensory experiences by encouraging children to manipulate many kinds of materials—blocks, puzzles; paints, glue, paper, and found materials: sand, water and dirt, musical instruments and measurement devices. They also provide many opportunities for projects, such as cooking, gardening, carpentry, and dramatic play. The hands-on approach to the education of six-, seven-, and eight-year-olds, as well as younger children, is strongly endorsed by the National Association for the Education of Young Children (NAEYC). The philosophy is clearly presented in NAEYC's *Developmentally Appropriate Practices (DAP) in Early Childhood Programs Serving Children from Birth through Eight.*

Play continues to be one of the most important activities for fostering cognitive development in the early grades. It is also a major route to enhancing social development and all other developmental skills. For the most part, six-, seven-, and eight-year-olds play well with other children, especially if the group is not too large. There is keen interest in making friends, being a friend, and having friends. At the same time, there also may be quarreling, bossing, and excluding: "If you play with Lynette, then you're not *my* friend." Some children show considerable aggression, but it often tends to be verbal, aimed at hurting feelings rather than causing physical harm.

Friends are usually playmates that the child has ready access to in the neighborhood and at school. Friends often are defined as someone who is "fun," "pretty," or "strong," or who "acts nice." Friendships at this age are easily established and readily abandoned; few are stable or long-lasting.

Throughout the primary school years, many children seem almost driven by the need to do everything right. On the other hand, they enjoy being challenged and completing tasks. They also like to make recognizable products and to join in organized activities. Most children enjoy these early school years. They become comfortable with themselves, their parents, and their teachers.

Primary school children tend to play
well together.

THE SIX-YEAR-OLD

New and exciting adventures begin to open up to six-year-olds as their coordination improves and their size and strength increase. New challenges often are met with a mixture of enthusiasm and frustration. Six-year-olds typically have difficulty making choices, and, at times, are overwhelmed by unfamiliar situations. At the same time, changes in their cognitive abilities enable them to see rules as useful for understanding everyday events and the behavior of others.

For many children, this period also marks the beginning of formal, subject-oriented schooling (it should be noted that formal academic activities at this age are considered developmentally inappropriate by many early childhood educators). Behavior problems or signs of tension, such as tics, nail-biting, or bed-wetting may flair up. Generally, these pass as children become familiar with new expectations and responsibilities associated with going to school. Despite the turmoil and trying times (for adults as well), most six-year-olds experience an abundance of good times marked by a lively curiosity, an eagerness to learn, an endearing sense of humor, and exuberant outbursts of affection and good will.

DEVELOPMENTAL PROFILES AND GROWTH PATTERNS

Growth and Physical Characteristics

- Growth occurs slowly, but steadily.
- Height increases 2 to 3 inches (5–7.5 cm) each year: girls are an average of 42 to 46 inches (105–115 cm) tall, boys, 44 to 47 inches (110–117.5 cm).
- Weight increases 5 to 7 pounds (2.3–3.2 kg) a year: girls weigh approximately 38 to 47 pounds (19.1–22.3 kg), boys, 42 to 49 pounds (17.3–21.4 kg).
- Weight gains reflect significant increases in muscle mass.
- Heart rate (80 beats per minute) and respiratory rates (18–28 breaths per minute) are similar to those of adults; rates vary with activity.
- Body takes on a lanky appearance as long bones of the arms and legs begin a phase of rapid growth.
- Loses "baby" (deciduous) teeth; permanent (secondary) teeth erupt, beginning with the two upper front teeth; girls tend to lose teeth at an earlier age than boys.
- Visual acuity should be 20/20; children testing 20/40 or less should have a professional evaluation.
- Farsightedness is not uncommon, often due to immature development (shape) of the eyeball.
- Facial features become more adult-like.
- Requires approximately 1,600 to 1,700 calories per day.

Motor Development

- Has increased muscle strength; typically, boys are stronger than girls of similar size.
- Gains greater control over large and fine motor skills; movements are more precise and deliberate, though some clumsiness persists.
- Enjoys vigorous physical activity: running, jumping, climbing, and throwing.
- Moves constantly, even when trying to sit still.
- Has increased dexterity and eye–hand coordination along with improved motor functioning which facilitates learning to ride a bicycle, swim, swing a bat, or kick a ball.
- Enjoys art projects: likes to paint, model with clay, "make things," draw and color, work with wood.
- Writes numbers and letters with varying degrees of precision and interest; may reverse or confuse certain letters: *b/d, p/g, g/q, t/f.*
- Traces around hand and other objects.
- Folds and cuts paper into simple shapes.
- Ties own shoes (still a struggle for some children).

6-YEAR-OLDS

Learning to ride a bicycle is a major
accomplishment.

Perceptual and Cognitive Development

- Span of attention increases; works at tasks for longer periods of time, though concentrated effort is not always consistent.
- Understands concepts, such as simple time markers (today, tomorrow, yesterday) or uncomplicated concepts of motion (cars go faster than bicycles).
- Recognizes seasons and major holidays and the activities associated with each.
- Enjoys the challenge of puzzles, counting and sorting activities, paper-and-pencil mazes, and games that involve matching letters and words with pictures.
- Recognizes some words by sight; attempts to sound out words (some children may be reading well by this time).

"This is my left hand."

- Identifies familiar coins: pennies, nickels, dimes, quarters.
- Can hold up and correctly name right and left hands fairly consistently.
- Clings to certain beliefs involving magic or fantasy: the Tooth Fairy swapping a coin for a tooth; Santa Claus bringing gifts.
- Arrives at some understanding about death and dying; often expresses fear that parents may die, especially mother.

Speech and Language Development

- Loves to talk, often nonstop; may be described as a chatterbox.
- Able to carry on adult-like conversations; asks many questions.
- Learns as many as five to ten new words each day; vocabulary consists of ten thousand to fourteen thousand words.
- Uses appropriate verb tenses, word order, and sentence structure.
- Uses language rather than tantrums or physical aggression to express displeasure: "That's mine! Give it back, you dummy."
- Talks self through steps required in simple problem-solving situations (though the "logic" may be unclear to adults).
- Imitates slang and profanity; finds "bathroom" talk extremely funny.
- Delights in telling jokes and riddles; often, the humor is far from subtle.
- Enjoys being read to and making up stories.
- Capable of learning more than one language; does so spontaneously in a bi- or multilingual family.

Loves to talk silly and make up jokes.

6-YEAR-OLDS

Personal-Social Development

- Experiences sudden mood swings: may be "best of friends" one minute, "worst of enemies" the next; loving one day, uncooperative and irritable the next; especially unpredictable toward mother or primary caregiver.
- Less dependent on parents as friendship circle expands; still needs closeness and nurturing, yet has urges to break away and "grow up."
- Anxious to please; needs and seeks adult approval, reassurance, and praise; may complain excessively about minor hurts to gain more attention.
- Continues to be self-centered (egocentric); still sees events almost entirely from own perspective: views everything and everyone as there for child's own benefit.
- Easily disappointed and frustrated by self-perceived failure.
- Cannot tolerate being corrected or losing at games; often goes "all to pieces": may sulk, cry, refuse to play, or reinvent rules to suit own purposes.
- Enthusiastic and inquisitive about surroundings and everyday events.
- Little or no understanding of ethical behavior or moral standards; often fibs, cheats, or "steals" objects belonging to others.
- Knows when he or she has been "bad"; values of "good" and "bad" are based on expectations and rules of parents and teachers.
- May be increasingly fearful of thunderstorms, the dark, unidentified noises, dogs and other animals.

6-YEAR-OLDS

DAILY ROUTINES—SIX-YEAR-OLDS

Eating

- Has a good appetite most of the time; often takes larger helpings than is able to finish. May skip an occasional meal; usually makes up for it later.
- Willingness to try new foods is unpredictable; has strong food preferences and definite dislikes.
- Table manners often are deplorable by adult standards; may revert to eating with fingers; stuffs mouth; continues to spill milk or drop food in lap.
- Has difficulty using table knife for cutting and fork for anything but spearing food.
- Finds it difficult to sit through an entire meal; wiggles and squirms, gets off (or "falls" off) chair, drops utensils.

continued

Toileting, Bathing, Dressing

- Balks at having to take a bath; finds many excuses for delaying or avoiding a bath entirely.
- Manages toileting routines without much help; sometimes is in a hurry or waits too long so that "accidents" happen.
- May revert to soiling or wetting pants during the first few weeks of school.
- Usually sleeps through the night without having to get up to use the bathroom. *Note:* Some children, especially boys, may not maintain a dry bed for another year or so.
- Careless about handwashing, bathing, and other self-care routines; needs frequent supervision and demonstrations to make sure they are carried out properly.
- Interested in selecting own clothes; needs subtle guidance in determining combinations and seasonal appropriateness.

Forgetful about caring for clothing.

- Drops clothing on floor or bed, loses shoes around the house, flings jacket down and often forgets where it is.

Sleeping

- Needs nine to eleven hours of uninterrupted sleep.
- Usually sleeps through the night; some children continue to have nightmares.
- May need night-light, special blanket, or favorite stuffed toy (sometimes all three).
- Finds numerous ways to avoid bedtime; when finally in bed, falls asleep quickly.
- If awake before parents, usually finds ways to amuse self with books, toys, or coloring.

continued

6-YEAR-OLDS

Play and Social Activities

- Strong sense of self is evident in terms of preferences and dislikes; uncompromising about wants and needs (often these do not coincide with adult plans or desires).
- Possessive about toys and books, parents and friends, but is able to share on some occasions.
- May have close, friendly relationship with one or two other children (often slightly older); play involves working together toward specific goals.
- Intolerant of being told what to do; may revert to tantrums.
- Eager for teacher's attention, praise, reassurance; now views teacher (rather than parent) as the ultimate source of "truth."

LEARNING ACTIVITIES

Tips for parents and caregivers:

- Provide materials for coloring, cutting, pasting, painting (paper chains are always big, regardless of the season).
- Offer paper-and-pencil games: dot-to-dot, number-to-number, find-the-embedded items; copying and tracing activities.
- Provide (and frequently join in) simple card games (Hearts, Old Maid) and board games, especially those where competitiveness can be played down.
- Keep a plentiful supply of books on hand for the child to read and look at as well as for the adult to read to the child.
- Allow collecting of objects according to child's own interest and system (which may make little sense to the adult).
- Make interesting dress-up clothes available for boys as well as girls; encourage housekeeping play and role-playing: teacher, pilot, hunter, plumber.
- Encourage simple cooking, carpentry, and construction activities with blocks, cars, trucks, planes, zoo, and farm animals. (Avoid battery-driven and other mechanical toys—once the novelty has worn off they offer little involvement, hence little learning.)
- Encourage bicycling, roller skating, swimming, experimenting on monkey bars; digging, throwing, catching, and batting activities.

6-YEAR-OLDS

DEVELOPMENTAL ALERTS

Check with a health care provider or early childhood specialist if, by the seventh birthday, the child *does not:*

- Show signs of ongoing growth: increasing height and weight; continuing motor development, such as running, jumping, balancing.
- Show some interest in reading and trying to reproduce letters, especially own name.
- Follow simple, multiple-step directions: "Finish your book, put it on the shelf, and then get your coat on."
- Follow through with instructions and complete simple tasks: putting dishes in the sink, picking up clothes, finishing a puzzle. *Note:* All children forget. Task incompletion is not a problem unless a child *repeatedly* leaves tasks unfinished.
- Begin to develop alternatives to excessive use of inappropriate behaviors in order to get own way.
- Develop a steady decrease in tension-type behaviors that may have developed with starting school: repeated grimacing or facial tics; eye twitching; grinding of teeth; regressive soiling or wetting; frequent stomachaches; refusing to go to school.

THE SEVEN-YEAR-OLD

Seven-year-olds are becoming more aware of themselves as individuals. They work hard at being responsible, being "good," and doing it "right." They tend to take themselves seriously—too seriously at times. When they fail to live up to their own self-imposed expectations, they may sulk or become withdrawn. It's as if children at seven are trying to think things through, integrate what they already know with the flood of new experiences coming their way. Worrying about what may or may not come to pass is also typical; for example, anticipating yet dreading second grade can create anxiety. Maybe the work will be too hard; maybe the teacher won't be "nice"; maybe the other kids won't be friendly.

At the same time, children of this age have many positive traits. They are more reasonable and willing to share and cooperate. They are becoming better listeners and better at understanding and following through on what they hear. They are able to stay on-task for longer periods of time. They strive mightily to do everything perfectly (which only increases their worry load). Because of these complicated feelings, parents and teachers need to accept the mood swings. It seems the moods reflect the child's overwhelming efforts to cope with the conflicts inherent in being a seven-year-old.

DEVELOPMENTAL PROFILES AND GROWTH PATTERNS

Growth and Physical Characteristics

- Weight increase tends to be relatively small; a gain of 6 pounds (2.7 kg) per year is typical. Seven-year-olds weigh approximately 50 to 55 pounds (22.7–25 kg).
- Height increases an average of 2.5 inches (6.25 cm) per year. Girls are approximately 44 to 44.5 inches (110 to 116.3 cm) tall, boys, 46 to 49.5 inches (115–124 cm).
- Muscle mass is fairly equal for boys and girls.
- Physical growth goes along slowly and steadily; a few girls may overtake some boys in height.
- Posture is more erect; arms and legs continuing to lengthen, giving a longer, leaner look to many seven-year-olds.
- Energy level comes and goes, fluctuating between spurts of high energy and intervals of temporary fatigue.
- May have a number of colds and other minor illnesses; these occur less frequently than at age six.
- Eyeballs continue to change shape and size; vision should be checked periodically to ensure good sight.
- Hair often grows darker in color.
- Baby teeth continue to be replaced by permanent teeth.

Motor Development

- Large and fine motor control more finely tuned: balances on either foot, runs up and down stairs with alternating feet, throws and catches smaller balls, practices batting balls.
- Tends to be cautious in undertaking the more challenging physical activities, such as climbing up or jumping down from high places.
- Often practices a new motor skill over and over until mastered, then drops it to work on something else.
- Sprawls prone on the floor while reading or watching television, propped up on one elbow, knees bent, feet and legs constantly waving back and forth or pumping up and down.
- Uses knife and fork appropriately, but inconsistently.
- Holds pencil in a tight grasp near the tip; rests head on forearm, lowers head almost to the table top when doing pencil-and-paper tasks.

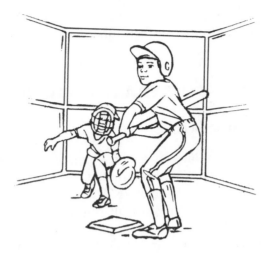

Practices batting.

- Produces letters and numbers in a deliberate and confident fashion: characters are increasingly uniform in size and shape; may run out of room on line or page when writing.

Perceptual and Cognitive Development

- Concepts of space and time becoming both logical and more practical: a year is "a long time"; a hundred miles is "far away."
- Beginning to grasp Piaget's concepts of conservation: for example, the shape of a container does not necessarily reflect the quantity it can hold.
- Has a better understanding of cause and effect: "If I'm late for school again, I'll be in big trouble."
- Can tell time by the clock and also understands calendar time—days, months, years, and seasons.
- Plans ahead: "I'm saving this cookie for tonight."
- Fascinated with magic tricks; enjoys putting on "shows" for parents and friends.
- Reading becomes easier; many seven-year-olds read for their own pleasure and enjoy retelling story details.
- Spelling ability not necessarily on a par with reading skills.
- Great interest in counting and saving money.
- Letter reversals and sound substitution still common in some children.

Speech and Language Development

- Enjoys storytelling; likes to write short stories, tell imaginative tales.
- Uses adult-like sentence structure and language in conversation; patterns reflect cultural and geographical differences.

Interested in saving money.

- Language becoming more precise and elaborate; greater use of descriptive adjectives and adverbs.
- Uses gestures to illustrate conversations.
- Verbally critical of own performances: "I didn't draw that right," "Her picture is better than mine."
- Verbal exaggeration commonplace: "I ate ten hot dogs at the picnic."
- May explain happenings in terms of own preferences or needs: "It didn't rain because I was going on a picnic."
- Describes personal experiences in great detail: "First we parked the car, then we hiked up this long trail, then we sat down on a broken tree near a lake and ate. . . ."
- Understands and carries out multiple-step instructions (up to five steps); may

"The cat was this big!"

need to have directions repeated because of not listening to entire request the first time.

- Enjoys writing simple letters to friends.

Personal-Social Development

- More outgoing; sees humor in everyday happenings; is cooperative and affectionate toward adults, less frequently annoyed with them.
- Likes to be the "teacher's helper"; eager for teacher's attention and approval, but less obvious about seeking it.
- Friends are important, but can find plenty to do if a friend is not available.
- Less quarrelsome, though squabbles and tattling continue to occur in both one-on-one and group play.
- Complains that family decisions are unjust; that a particular sibling gets to do more or is given more.
- Often blames others for own mistakes; makes up alibis for personal shortcomings: "I could have made a better one, but my teacher didn't give me enough time."
- Same-gender playmates and play groups predominate.
- Feelings easily hurt; may worry about not being liked; may cry, be embarrassed, or state adamantly, "I will never play with you again" when criticized.
- Takes responsibilities seriously; can be trusted to carry out directions and commitments; worries about being late for school or not getting work done.

DAILY ROUTINES—SEVEN-YEAR-OLDS

Eating

- Eats most foods; better about sampling unfamiliar foods or taking small tastes of disliked foods, but still refuses a few strong "hates."
- Interested in food; likes to help with grocery shopping and meal preparation.
- Table manners far from perfect, but improving; less spilled milk and other "accidents" due to silliness or haste to finish.
- Uses eating utensils with relative ease; seldom eats with fingers; some children still have trouble cutting meat.
- Less dawdling over meals, though easily distracted by things going on elsewhere in the house or outdoors.

continued

Toileting, Bathing, Dressing

- May dillydally at bathtime; once in the tub, seems to enjoy the experience; can manage own bath with a minimum of help.
- Dresses self; dawdling continues, but child can speed up when time becomes critical.
- Capable of buttoning and zipping; ties own shoes; often careless: buttons askew, shoe laces soon dragging.
- Clothes not a major interest; wears whatever is laid out or available.
- Both boys and girls becoming more interested in combing or brushing their own hair.
- Good bowel and bladder control; individual rhythm well established; may resist having bowel movements at school.
- Less likely to get up during the night to use the toilet.

Often needs reminding about tying shoes.

Sleeping

- Averages ten to eleven hours of sleep at night; children who are in bed fewer hours, often have trouble getting up in the morning.
- Sleeps soundly with few if any bad dreams; instead, often dreams about own exploits and adventures.
- Can get ready for bed independently most nights, but wants to be tucked in or read to.
- Often wakes up early; occupies self in bed with toys, counting out savings in piggy-bank, looking at baseball card collection, reading.

Enjoys reading in bed.

Play and Social Activities

- Participates in organized group activities (Boys' and Girls' Clubs, Cub Scouts and Brownies, swim and soccer teams).

7-YEAR-OLDS

continued

Eager to join organized groups.

- Does not want to miss school or scheduled events; wants to "keep up" with friends and classmates.
- Interested in coloring and cutting things out, with a friend or alone.
- Favorite play activities include bicycle riding, climbing activities, and computer games.
- Eager to play competitive board and card games, but may "bend" the rules when losing.

7-YEAR-OLDS

LEARNING ACTIVITIES

Tips for parents and caregivers:

- Make trips to the library for children's story time and dramatic play activities as well as books.
- Sign up for free or low-cost community offerings of interest to the child: art, science, swimming, dancing.
- Take family "collecting walks" in the neighborhood, on nearby beaches, or in parks; support child's efforts to organize "treasures."
- Accumulate tools and equipment that really work: simple carpentry and garden tools, science materials (growing a potato vine, maintaining an ant farm or a simple aquarium.

- Gather materials for creating art projects, models, science experiments: pieces of wood, plastic, various weights and textures of cardboard and paper, beads, fabric, yarn.
- Offer dress-up clothes and props for planning and staging "shows"; attend the performances.
- Provide doll house, farm or zoo set, service station or airport, complete with small-scale people, animals, and equipment.

 ## DEVELOPMENTAL ALERTS

Check with a health care provider or early childhood specialist if, by the eighth birthday, the child *does not:*

- Attend to the task at hand; show longer periods of sitting quietly, listening, responding appropriately.
- Follow through on simple instructions.
- Go to school willingly most days (of concern are excessive complaints about stomachaches or headaches when getting ready for school).
- Make friends (observe closely to see if the child plays alone most of the time or withdraws consistently from contact with other children).
- Sleep soundly most nights (frequent and recurring nightmares or bad dreams are usually at a minimum at this age).
- Seem to see or hear adequately at times (squints, rubs eyes excessively, asks frequently to have things repeated).
- Handle stressful situations without undue emotional upset (excessive crying, sleeping or eating disturbances, withdrawal, frequent anxiety).
- Assume responsibility for personal care (dressing, bathing, feeding self) most of the time.
- Show improved motor skills.

8-YEAR-OLDS

THE EIGHT-YEAR-OLD

Eight-year-olds display a great enthusiasm for life. Energy is concentrated on improving skills they already possess and enhancing what they already know. Eight-year-olds once again experience strong feelings of independence and are eager to make decisions about their own plans and friends. Interests and attention are increasingly devoted to peers and team or group activities rather than parents, teachers, or siblings. Sometime near midyear, boys and girls go their separate ways and form new interests in same-gender groups.

DEVELOPMENTAL PROFILES AND GROWTH PATTERNS

Growth and Physical Characteristics

- Continues to gain 5 to 7 pounds (2.3–3.2 kg) per year; an eight-year-old weighs approximately 55 to 61 pounds (25–27.7 kg). Girls typically weigh less than boys.
- Height continues to increase at a pace that is slow but steady. Grows an average of 2.5 inches (6.25 cm) per year; girls are often taller (46 to 49 inches [115–122.5 cm]) as compared to boys (48 to 52 inches [120–130 cm]).
- Body shape takes on a more mature appearance; arms and legs grow longer, creating an image that is tall and lanky.
- Normal vision acuity is 20/20. Vision should be checked periodically to ensure good sight.
- Some girls may begin to develop breasts and pubic hair, and experience menses.
- Mood swings may become more apparent as changes in hormonal activity occur.
- Overall state of health improves; experiences fewer illnesses.

Motor Development

- Enjoys vigorous activity; likes to dance, roller blade, swim, wrestle, ride bikes, and fly kites.
- Seeks out opportunities to participate in team activities and games, such as soccer, baseball, and kickball.
- Exhibits significant improvement in agility, balance, speed, and strength.
- Copies words and numbers from blackboard with increasing speed and accuracy; has good eye–hand coordination.
- Seems to possess endless energy.

Perceptual and Cognitive Development

- Collects objects; organizes and displays items according to more complex systems; bargains and trades with friends to obtain additional pieces.
- Eager to save money for small purchases; develops plans to earn cash for odd jobs; studies catalogues and magazines for ideas of items to purchase.
- Beginning to take an interest in what others think and do; understands there are differences of opinion, cultures, distant countries.

8-YEAR-OLDS

Writes letters with imaginative detail.

- Accepts challenge and responsibility with enthusiasm; delights in being asked to perform tasks, both at home and in school; interested in being rewarded for efforts.
- Likes to read and work independently; spends considerable time planning and making lists.
- Understands perspective (shadow, distance, shape); drawings reflect more realistic portrayal of objects.
- Begins to understand elementary principles of conservation: while jars that are tall and narrow may look different from those that are short and wide, they may hold the same amount.
- Uses more sophisticated logic in efforts to understand everyday events; for example, is systematic in looking for a misplaced jacket or toy.
- Adds and subtracts multiple-digit numbers; learning multiplication and division.
- Looks forward to school and is disappointed when ill or unable to attend.

Speech and Language Development

- Delights in telling jokes and riddles.
- Understands and carries out multiple-step instructions (up to five steps); may need to have directions repeated because of not listening to the entire request.
- Enjoys writing letters to friends; includes descriptions that are imaginative and detailed.
- Uses language to criticize and compliment others; repeats slang and curse words.
- Understands and follows rules of grammar in conversation and written form.
- Intrigued with learning secret word codes and using code language.
- Converses fluently with adults; able to think and talk about past and future: "What time are we leaving to get to the swim meet next week?"

8-YEAR-OLDS

Personal-Social Development

- Forming opinions; about moral values and attitudes; declares things either right or wrong.
- Plays with two or three "best" friends, most often of the same age and gender; also enjoys spending some time alone.
- Less critical of own performance, but is easily frustrated and upset when unable to complete a task or when the product does not meet expectations.
- Enjoys team games and activities; group membership and acceptance by peers are important.
- Still blames others or makes up alibis to explain own shortcomings or mistakes.
- Enjoys talking on the telephone with friends.
- Understands and respects the fact that some children are more talented in certain areas, such as drawing, sports, reading, art, or music.
- Still desires attention and recognition from teacher or parents; enjoys performing for adults and challenging them in games.

DAILY ROUTINES—EIGHT-YEAR-OLDS

Eating

- Most have a hearty appetite; boys typically eat more than girls.
- Enjoys eating; willing to try new foods and some of the foods previously refused.
- Takes pride in using good table manners, especially when eating out or when company is present; at home, manners of less concern.
- May stuff mouth with too much food or not chew food thoroughly in order to finish meal quickly to get back to previous activities.

Toileting, Bathing, Dressing

- Has an established pattern for bowel and bladder functions; usually has good control, but may need to urinate more frequently when under stress.
- Handwashing often hurried; dirt tends to end up on towel rather than down the drain.
- Enjoys bath and playing in water; easily sidetracked when supposed to be getting ready to bathe; some children are able to prepare their own bath.
- Takes greater interest in appearance, selecting and coordinating own outfits, brushing hair, and looking good.

continued

8-YEAR-OLDS

OBSERVING CHILDREN

What we know about children, how they grow, how they learn, how they interact with others, stems from first-hand observation. Early psychologists and educators such as Froebel, Pestalozzi, Freud, Montessori, Gesell, Skinner, and Piaget observed the daily activities of hundreds of infants and children. They recorded what they saw and heard as the children learned to walk and talk, identify shapes and colors, recognize numbers and letters, get along with others, reason, and solve problems. These recorded observations provide the foundation for what we now know about child development, effective teaching, curriculum models, and the significance of the parent-child relationship.

TEACHERS AS CLASSROOM OBSERVERS

The benchmark of a quality early childhood program is regularly scheduled observations and frequent notetaking by the adults. Watching and recording what children actually do in the classroom and in the outdoor play area enables staff to design appropriate indoor and outdoor learning environments.

Teachers' observations are critical. They are trained in child development. They know what to expect of children. They can apply their knowledge effectively in an environment where children are "being themselves" and plan for the individual needs and differences among children.

At parent conferences, teachers rely on their observation records to cite concrete examples related to the child's progress. Written observations attest to the teacher's interest in each child and to the teacher's ability to communicate that interest to parents.

PARENTS AS CLASSROOM OBSERVERS

Parents must always be welcome in their child's classroom, whether as scheduled observers or on a drop-in basis. They have a right to see and question everything that occurs in the classroom and outside play area. When parents come for a scheduled observation; they can be given a clipboard and paper so they can make notes about whatever interests them; for example, what and whom their child plays with, or what seems to please or bother their child. In a follow-up discussion, teachers can learn how parents view the program and can explore mutual concerns and pleasure about the child's progress.

Parents' observations, made at home or at school, are invaluable. Parents know their child better than anyone else. They see their child under every imaginable circumstance. They are aware of the child's likes and dislikes, joys and anxieties. Most importantly, they know what they want for their child.

TYPES OF OBSERVATIONS

Recorded observations take many
forms: anecdotal notes, running records
and logs, samples of children's speech
and language, frequency count and
duration measures. Checklists and rating scales also rely on direct observations. A brief sampling of observation
methods is given here. The annotated
bibliography (Appendix 5) provides references for additional information.

Anecdotal Notes

Anecdotal notes are made on a small
note pad (3 X 5 inches) carried in a
pocket. The notes are brief, dated
phrases about discrete behaviors
observed in a given child. The notes can
be used to track development in specific domains or to gather information
about a specific concern. Teachers take
a minute or less several times a day to
write down a few relevant words about
what they see happening. Over time,
the dated notes yield a composite picture. It may point to a need for special
guidance plans. If so, continuing the
notetaking enables teachers to see if
the plan is helping the child. If there
are no particular concerns, anecdotal
notes, filed chronologically by developmental domains, are essential to plac-
ing a child, writing progress reports,
and preparing for parent conferences.

Language Samples

To obtain a language sample, an observer writes down every utterance a child makes, exactly as the child says it. One purpose of the samplings, usually done over a month or so for 15 or 20 minutes at a time, is to track the child's speech and language development. Another purpose is to see if the child's language "works." Is the child communicating effectively? Does the child get what he or she needs and wants by using language? No other behaviors (except communicative gestures or facial grimaces)

are recorded, though brief notations might be made; for example, that children rarely respond to the child's verbal overtures. Language samples are invaluable in planning individualized programs. They also are essential in preparing for parent conferences, which can be enlivened when teachers read amusing quips or insightful statements made by the child.

Frequency and Duration Counts

When concerns arise about a specific aspect of a child's behavior, teachers must first determine how often the behavior occurs (frequency) or how long it goes on (duration). Such counts are easily made while teachers carry out their other responsibilities. One type of frequency count simply requires the teacher to make a tally mark every time the child engages in the specified behavior. A count may reveal, for example, that a two-year-old who was said to cry or hit "all the time" was actually doing so only once or twice a morning, some mornings not at all. For behaviors that occur at a high rate, teachers sometimes carry a golf stroke or knitting stitch counter.

A duration count (or measure) often consists of simply jotting down the time a child enters and leaves an area or activity. Another example would be penciling (unobtrusively) on a corner of a painting or collage the time the child started and finished the project. These are but two examples of easy-to-make observations. A frequency count provides significant information as to whether a "problem" is really a

problem. A duration count helps teachers decide if they need to try to enhance the child's span of attention in certain program areas.

Checklists

Checklists allow a teacher or other observer to quickly record the occurrence of a specified behavior or developmental achievement. In infant centers, many "firsts" can be checked off: the day Josie first smiled, rolled over, walked alone. In preschools, a checklist with children's names down one side and curriculum objectives across the top is useful. By inserting the date, teachers "check off" when Carmen correctly identified and matched the primary colors; John J. built a tower of eight one-inch cubes; Arden zipped her jacket by herself. Checklists often are constructed by teachers to reflect program objectives. The lists, whether teacher-made or commercial, can be simple or detailed, depending on need (examples: Appendix 2).

OBJECTIVITY WHEN OBSERVING

Objectivity means writing down only what the child actually does and says. It means that any two observers (two teachers, a teacher and a parent, a volunteer and an aide), observing the same child at the same time, produce identical reports of what the child actually did.

Reality-based information is essential for several reasons:

• It provides facts (not personal bias) in determining the extent to which a problem affects the child's developmental progress or the well-being of other children.

• It provides consensus and a firm base for arranging individualized learning activities.

• It is essential in tracking a child's progress in all developmental areas.

• It provides concrete information for conducting effective parent-teacher conferences.

- Helps care for own clothes; hangs clothes up most times, helps with laundry by folding and returning items to dresser.
- Skilled at tying shoes, but often can't be bothered.

Sleeping

- Sleeps soundly through the night (averages ten hours); efforts to delay bedtime may suggest less sleep is needed.
- Begins to question established bedtime; wants to stay up later; dawdles, becomes distracted while getting ready for bed.
- May wake early and get dressed while family members are still sleeping.

Play and Social Activities

- Enjoys competitive activities and sports (soccer, baseball, swimming, gymnastics); eager to join a team; just as eager to quit if too much forced competition.
- May adopt a know-it-all attitude toward the end of the eighth year; becomes argumentative with peers (and adults).
- Likes to play board, electronic, and card games; often interprets rules so as to improve own chances of winning.
- Eager for acceptance from peers; begins to imitate clothing fads, hairstyles, behavior, and language of admired peers.

LEARNING ACTIVITIES

Tips for parents and caregivers:

- Provide (and join in) games that require a moderate degree of strategy: checkers, dominoes, card games, magic sets, computer games.
- Encourage creativity; provide materials for simple painting, crafts, cooking, or building projects.
- Make frequent trips to the library; provide books to read, as well as stories on audio- and videocassettes.
- Invest in an inexpensive camera; encourage children to experiment.
- Arrange for opportunities to develop skills in noncompetitive activities—swimming, dancing, tumbling, skating, skiing, musical instruments; this is a time of *trying out* many interests; seldom is there a long-term commitment.
- Assign routine tasks, such as feeding the dog, folding laundry, or setting the dinner table to foster a sense of responsibility.

8-YEAR-OLDS

DEVELOPMENTAL ALERTS

Check with a health care provider or early childhood specialist if, by the ninth birthday, the child *does not:*

- Exhibit a good appetite and continued weight gain (some children, especially girls, may already begin to show early signs of an eating disorder).
- Experience fewer illnesses.
- Show improved motor skills, in terms of agility, speed, and balance.
- Understand abstract concepts and use complex thought processes to problem-solve.
- Enjoy school and the challenge of learning.
- Follow through on multiple-step instructions.
- Express ideas clearly and fluently.
- Form friendships with other children and enjoy participating in group activities.

THE NEXT FEW YEARS

Between eight and twelve years of age, friendships become more enduring, with mutual understanding and respect. Ways of thinking about themselves, others, and the world in general change dramatically. During this period, the child learns more abstract ways of thinking, gains greater understanding about cause and effect, and begins to use genuine logic in figuring out how things work. The child also comprehends that things really are the same in spite of being used for alternative purposes or seen from a different perspective—a shovel can be used not only for digging, but for prying; a soup bowl can be traced around to draw a circle.

The stretch of years from eight to early adolescence is usually enjoyable and fairly peaceful for all concerned. The child has adjusted to being at school for six or more hours each day. The stresses, strains, and frustrations of learning to read, write, do basic arithmetic, and follow directions are long forgotten. Changes in physical growth and development are quite different from child to child during this period. Girls in particular grow more rapidly. Research finds girls as young as eight or nine may already be experiencing some of the early hormonal changes associated with puberty.

And so, the era of childhood comes to an end. The years have been a time of dramatic changes. There has been the wondrous evolvement from a small, helpless infant into an adult-like individual capable of complex and highly coordinated motor, cognitive, language, and social behaviors.

Test Your Knowledge

REVIEW QUESTIONS

1. List one characteristic that describes the typical cognitive skill of a six-year-old, a seven-year-old, and an eight-year-old.

   a.

   b.

   c.

2. List three perceptual skills that indicate readiness to begin reading.

   a.

   b.

   c.

3. List three reasonable expectations for a six-year-old in terms of home routines.

   a.

   b.

   c.

4. List three developmentally appropriate activities that a parent or teacher might utilize to expand the language skills of seven- and eight-year-olds.

   a.

   b.

   c.

5. List three warning signs that an eight-year-old might need to be seen by a health care provider or early childhood specialist.

   a.

   b.

   c.

TRUE OR FALSE

1. Increased muscle mass is significantly related to weight gain in six-year-olds.

2. Most seven-year-olds are able to take care of their own personal needs—bathing, dressing, eating—without assistance.

3. Eight-year-olds become quite skilled at understanding another's point of view.

4. Playing with blocks, sand, water, and housekeeping activities should be eliminated from a primary school curriculum.

5. Seven-year-olds tend to worry about what might happen.

6. Team membership is not a realistic expectation for the typical seven- or eight-year-old.

7. Eight-year-olds show no concept of logical thinking.

8. Some evidence of abstract or logical thinking is seen in most six-, seven-, and eight-year-olds.

9. Seven- and eight-year-olds have a good appetite and will usually try foods that are served.

10. A riddle book, soccer ball, and stamp collecting kit would make appropriate gifts for an eight-year-old.

MULTIPLE CHOICE   *Select one or more correct answers from the lists below.*

1. An eight-year-old can be expected to

   a. respect the privacy of others.

   b. take care of younger brothers or sisters in parents' absence.

   c. get themselves and younger siblings ready for school without adult help or supervision.

2. Grammatical irregularities

   a. are not uncommon in six-year-olds.

   b. are a sign of abnormality; normally developing seven-year-olds would never be heard to say, "The mouses falled into the water."

   c. should always be corrected and the child made to practice the correct form by repeating it at least ten times.

3. Six-year-olds
    a. do a good bit of tattling and bossing.
    b. make lasting friendships.
    c. are seldom aggressive, either verbally or physically.

4. Seven-year-olds are
    a. extremely fussy about what they wear.
    b. frequently displeased with their own efforts.
    c. known for their consistently high energy level.

5. Which of the following is not typical behavior of an eight-year-old?
    a. assigning character names to friends and playing "Ninja turtles."
    b. organizing friends to help construct a spaceship from a large cardboard box.
    c. developmentally unready to participate in team games.

CHAPTER 8

WHEN TO SEEK HELP

Is my child all right? Most parents at one time or another ask this question during their child's infancy and early childhood years. Many caregivers and preschool teachers ask a similar question about the occasional child who seems somehow "different" from other children in the group. Such questions, raised by either parents or teachers, are a positive sign; they indicate concern for the child.

Young children, as emphasized in Chapter 1, vary greatly in their development. It is the rare child who is truly typical in every way. Many children experience developmental irregularities of one kind or another with no long-term negative effects. Other children with irregularities that appear no more threatening, may be at developmental risk. And what about the child who seems typical in many ways, yet is different enough to be of concern to parents and caregivers? The answer: any persistent question about a child's growth and behavior calls for prompt and thorough investigation.

Developmental problems or delays, whether suspected or obvious, must receive immediate attention. Years of research give conclusive evidence that early identification and **intervention** can lessen the seriousness of a problem. Early intervention can also reduce, or prevent, negative impact on other areas of development. Reliable screening programs for infants and young children from birth through age five and beyond are widely available. Federal legislation and money are available to assist in locating and treating young children with developmental problems. The screening programs are often community-sponsored or associated with public school systems.

Screening programs are designed to identify children who have or may be at-risk for developmental problems. Primarily, the focus is on hearing and vision, physical health, and development in general. The tests are designed to be easily administered so that large numbers of children can be assessed in their own communities through public health departments, Head Start programs, or child care centers. Without early screening, many children may not receive necessary services until they reach school

---

intervention—*Treatment or special services for infants and young children; it needs to be provided as early as possible to prevent complications or delays in development.*

age. By that time, if there is a problem, it often has become serious, requiring extensive therapy and special education. Many such outcomes can be avoided with early attention to the needs of the child and family.

A nationwide screening program is called *Child Find*. The goal of Child Find is to locate infants and children who have undiagnosed developmental problems or are at-risk for the onset of such problems. This federally funded program has two major purposes. One is to identify eligible children as early in life as possible in order to provide intervention. The second is to help families find diagnostic and early intervention services. Each state is required to establish a Child Find system.

Parents are usually the first to suspect a developmental problem or delay in their child. It is parents who become uneasy or fear that something is not quite right. Even so, they may not seek help immediately for a variety of reasons:

- Not knowing how to go about getting professional help.
- Anxiety about costs.
- Uneasiness about seeking advice on a suspected problem that often is difficult to identify or describe.
- Self-doubt arising from the unwitting assurance (perhaps from a well-meaning physician or relative) that there really is no problem or that the child will eventually "outgrow" whatever it is.
- Confusion or retreat when given conflicting, frightening, or incomprehensible clinical information.

**Signs of developmental
problems may be subtle.**

- Timidity about pressing for clarification, asking for a second opinion.
- Reluctance to openly acknowledge concern; in many cultures, such things are family matters, not to be made public.
- Denial that a problem even exists.

Consequently, the child's problem often does not go away; instead, it worsens. For this reason parents must always be encouraged to talk about their misgivings or doubts about their child's development. Health care professionals, teachers, caregivers—all who work or have contact with young children—must listen intently and respond seriously to any concern parents express, directly or indirectly.

IS THERE A PROBLEM?

Deciding if a developmental delay or irregularity is of serious concern is not always easy. Some problems are so obvious they can readily be identified: the child with Down syndrome is easily recognized because of unique physical characteristics. However, the basis for determining many other developmental problems is not always clear-cut. The signs may be so subtle, so difficult to pinpoint, that it is hard to clearly distinguish between children who definitely have a problem—the definite yes's—and those who definitely do not have a problem—the definite no's. The "may be"—is there or is there not a problem?—can be an even more complex issue.

To determine if a delay or deviation is of real concern, several factors may complicate the matter. For example:

- Children who exhibit signs of developmental problems in certain areas often continue to develop much like a typical child in other respects; such children present a confusing developmental profile.
- Great variation exists in the range of children's achievements within developmental areas and within the child; the rate of maturation is uneven and conditions in the child's environment are continually changing. Both maturation and environment interact to exert a strong influence on every aspect of the child's development.
- Family beliefs, values, and cultural background have significant influence on how parents raise their children. *Developmental milestones are not universal;* how they are perceived can vary from culture to culture, even from family to family. Respect for diverse family and community lifestyles is always a major consideration when gathering and interpreting information about a child's development. (See diversity insert.)
- Developmental delays or problems may not be immediately apparent. Many children learn to compensate for deficiencies, such as a mild to moderate vision

**Delay in acquiring basic skills may be
cause for concern.**

or hearing loss. It is not until later, when the child is placed in structured and more demanding situations, as in a first-grade reading class, that these deficiencies become obvious.

- **Intermittent** health problems can affect children's performance. For example, a child may have severe and recurring bouts of **otitis media** that appear to clear up completely between episodes. A hearing test given when the child is free of infection may show no hearing loss; the same child may be quite deaf when the infection is active. Intermittent periods of near-deafness, sometimes lasting a week or more, can result in long-term language and cognitive delays, even in severely challenging behaviors in some children.

At what point should a hunch or uncomfortable feeling about a child be a call for action? The answer is clear: Whenever parents feel uncertain about a child's developmental progress or lack of progress, they should seek help. Parents who are uneasy about their child need to discuss their concerns with an early childhood specialist or health care provider. Together they can determine if developmental screening is warranted. Certainly, a developmental delay or irregularity demands investigation whenever it interferes with a child's ability to participate in everyday activities. The frequent occurrence or constant repetition of a troublesome behavior is often a reliable sign that

---

intermittent—*Anything that comes and goes at intervals.*
otitis media—*Middle ear infection usually accompanied by pain and accumulation of fluid; most commonly experienced by children under six.*

Noting and recording a child's behavior
reveals what is actually occurring.

help should be sought. Seldom is a single incidence of a questionable behavior cause for concern. However, a child's continuing reluctance to attempt a new skill or to fully acquire a developmental skill should be a concern. For example, a ten-month-old infant who tries to sit alone, but still must use hands for support may or may not have a problem. However, clusters or groups of delays or developmental differences are always a warning sign: a ten-month-old infant who is not sitting without support and not smiling and babbling in response to others, almost surely is experiencing developmental difficulty. In either case, the need for developmental screening is indicated.

What do teachers and caregivers do when parents fail to express concern? Though it may be difficult in some instances, it is the staff's responsibility to discuss their concerns in a conference with the parents. In that setting, every effort is made to help parents accept that the child should be referred for evaluation. Under no circumstances may staff members bypass parents and do the referring themselves. Staff always can reassure parents, however, of their willingness to help find the necessary services.

EVALUATING THE YOUNG CHILD

Several levels of information-gathering are involved in a comprehensive developmental evaluation. These include observation and recording, screening, and diagnostic assessment. A combination of observation and screening techniques is useful for initial location and identification of individual children with possible delayed or at-risk development. Diagnostic assessment includes in-depth testing and professional interpretation of results. Clinicians from various disciplines should participate in the diagnosis. It is their responsibility to provide detailed information about areas of concern and the specific nature of the child's problems. For example, a four-year-old's delayed speech patterns may be noted during routine screening procedures. Subsequent diagnostic testing may pinpoint several other conditions: a moderate, **bilateral** hearing loss, a severe **malocclusion,** and withdrawn behaviors. Poor production of many letter sounds and an expressive vocabulary typical of a two-and-one-half-year-old may also be recorded. These clinical findings can be translated into educational strategies and intervention procedures that will benefit the child's overall development.

Observing and Recording

The evaluation process always begins with systematic observation. (See observation insert.) Noting and recording various aspects of a child's behavior enables the evaluator—parent, teacher, clinician—to focus on what is actually occurring. In other words, observations provide information about what the child can and cannot do at the time of the observation. Observational data can be obtained by using simple checklists, frequency counts (how often a specific behavior occurs), short written notations (anecdotal notes), or longer written narratives ("running records"). Duration measures provide information on how long a child engages in a particular behavior or stays with an activity.

Direct observation often confirms or rules out impressions or suspicions regarding a child's abilities. For example, a child may not count to 5 when asked to do so in a

Participating in a pure-tone audiometric test.

bilateral—Loss of hearing in both ears.
malocclusion—Poor alignment of the upper and lower jaws and teeth; often called overbite.

testing situation. That same child, however, may be observed to spontaneously and correctly count seven or eight objects while at play. A child thought to be hyperactive may be observed to sit quietly for five- to ten-minute stretches when given interesting and challenging activities, thereby ruling out hyperactivity. (*Note:* The term hyperactive is greatly overused and misused; it should not be used to describe or label any child unless so diagnosed by a developmental team.) Focusing on a child at play, alone or with other children, is especially revealing. No evaluation of a young child is truly valid without direct observations of that child at play in familiar surroundings.

Parents' observations are particularly valuable. They provide information and understanding that cannot be obtained from any other source. They also give insight into parents' attitudes, perceptions, and expectations concerning their child. Involving parents in the observation phase of evaluation may also help reduce their anxiety. Important, too, is the fact that direct observation often points up unrecognized strengths and abilities in a child. When parents actually see their child engaged in appropriate activities, it may encourage them to focus more on the child's strengths and less on the child's shortcomings.

Screening

In addition to direct observation, screening is an important step in identifying developmental problems. The purpose of screening tests is to determine if the child needs more comprehensive evaluation. Screening tests assess only current performance. They appraise general abilities as well as impairments or delays in fine and gross motor skills, cognition, speech and language development, and personal and social responsiveness. An overall picture of a child's development can be obtained through:

- a medical examination,
- vision and hearing evaluations,
- developmental checklists (Appendix 2),
- parents' responses to a developmental history (Appendix 3),
- an interview with parents.

If problems or suspected problems are noted during screening, clinically conducted diagnoses are indicated. *Note:* Screening tests *do not* serve as diagnosis; they *do not* predict future academic success; they *do not* constitute a basis for planning intervention programs.

Several questions should be asked when choosing a test:

- Is it appropriate for the child's age?
- Is it free of bias related to the child's economic, geographic, or cultural background?

- Can it be administered in the child's first language? If not, is a skilled interpreter available to assist the child and family?
- Is it reliable in isolating children who should be referred for further testing from those who do not?
- Is it simple and economical to administer?

Appendix 4 provides a sampling of widely used screening tests and a brief list of popular assessment instruments. Included are examples of **ecological** evaluations of home and school. Information about the child's everyday surroundings is essential in planning both prevention and intervention programs.

IQ Tests: Are They Appropriate for Young Children?

Intelligence tests, such as the Wechsler Intelligence Scale for Children (WISC) and the Stanford Binet Intelligence Scales, are sometimes administered to young children. They are *not* intended as screening instruments. Neither are they regarded by most early childhood specialists as appropriate tests for young children. IQ tests are mentioned here, however, because of their continued use in some screening situations. The

Vision screening is important for identifying problems.

Sound localization is useful for informal testing of the young child's hearing.

ecological—*Interrelationships between each living thing and the environments in which it functions.*

purpose of IQ tests is to attempt to determine a child's ability to process information. Scores received on an IQ test are compared to scores of other children of the same age. These tests try to measure how much the child knows, how well the child solves problems, and how quickly the child can perform a variety of cognitive tasks. IQ tests and the resulting scores must be used with caution, even skepticism, where young children are concerned.

The IQ scores of infants and preschool-age children *are not valid predictors* of future or even current intellectual performance. Especially, they do not predict how well a child will do in school. (The single best predictor of a child's school performance is the level of the mother's education!) Even though intelligence is influenced to some unknown degree by heredity and maturation, a child's achievement is not a developmental issue for a significant reason; IQ tests do not measure the opportunities the child has had to learn nor the quality of those learning experiences (as valuable as these things may be in the child's own culture). What the dominant culture says a child should know influences how well a child will score. Children raised in poverty, for example, or in non-English speaking homes often do not have the opportunity to acquire the specific kinds of information represented by the test items. Standardized IQ tests do not account for these factors. Therefore, the use of a single IQ test score to determine a child's cognitive or intellectual skills *must be challenged.*

Interpreting Test Results

The widespread use of screening programs is of great benefit in detecting possible developmental problems in children, but the findings are always open to question. The screening process itself can sometimes have a negative effect on the outcome. Young children's attention spans are short and vary considerably from day to day, or from task to task. Illness, fatigue, anxiety, lack of cooperation, irritability, or restlessness can have a negative effect on performance. Poor performance also may result when young children are unaccustomed to being tested or the person doing the testing. Often children are capable of doing much better in a familiar setting. Consequently, *results derived from screening assessments must be regarded with caution.* The following points serve as reminders for both both parents and teachers.

- Interpret and use test results with extreme caution. Avoid drawing hasty conclusions. Above all, do not accept a diagnosis from limited information or a single test score. In analyzing screening results, recognize that developmental test results are strictly a measure of the child's *abilities at that given moment.* They may not be an accurate representation of the child's actual development or developmental potential. Only periodic observation can provide a complete picture of the child's developing skills and abilities.
- Never underestimate the influence of home and family on a child's performance.

The more recent screening procedures are making a greater effort to promote family participation and to evaluate family concerns, priorities, and resources. There also is growing emphasis on screening in familiar environments where children feel more comfortable and secure.

- Recognize the dangers of labeling an individual child as learning disabled, mentally retarded, or behavior disorder on the basis of any one test. Remember, too, that labels are of little benefit. They can have a negative effect on both expectations for the child and ways that parents, caregivers, and teachers respond to the child.

- *Question test scores.* Test results can be interpreted incorrectly. One test may suggest that a child has a developmental delay when actually nothing is wrong. Such conclusions are called *false positives.* The opposite conclusion can also be reached. A child may have a problem that does not show up in the screening and so may be incorrectly identified as normal. This is a *false negative.* The first situation leads to unnecessary anxiety and disappointment for the child's family, even changes the way they respond to their child. The latter situation—the false negative—can lull a family into not seeking further help, and so the child's problem worsens. Both situations can be avoided with careful interpretation of screening test results.

- Results from screening tests *do not* constitute a diagnosis. Additional information must be collected and in-depth clinical testing must be completed before a diagnosis is given or confirmed. Even then, errors may occur in diagnosing developmental problems. There are many reasons for misdiagnosis, such as inconsistent and rapid changes in a child's growth and developmental achievements or changing environmental factors, such as divorce or family relocation.

- Failed items on a screening test do not indicate curriculum items or skills to be taught. The test skills are but single items representative of a broad range of skills to be expected in a given developmental area at an approximate age. A child who cannot stand on one foot for five seconds will not overcome a developmental problem by being taught to stand on one foot for a given time period. It should be stressed once again, that screening test items are not a suitable basis for constructing curriculum activities.

- Test results *do not* predict the child's developmental future. As stressed earlier, screening tests measure a child's abilities and achievements at the time of testing. In many cases, the results do not correlate with subsequent testing. There is always the need for ongoing observation, assessment, and in-depth clinical diagnosis when screening tests indicate potential problems and delays.

In the elementary grades, *achievement tests* are administered regularly by most school districts. These tests are designed to measure how much the child has been learning in school about specific subject areas. On such tests, the child is assigned a percentile ranking, based on a comparison with other children of the same grade level. For example, a child in the 50th percentile in math is doing as well as 50 percent of the children in the same grade. Again, test scores should be backed up by teachers' observations of children and by collected samples (portfolios) of children's work.

In conclusion, careful observation and developmental screening are integral parts of a comprehensive assessment of the young child. Such evaluations provide information about the status of the child, but only at the time of testing. Information obtained from observation and screening, when used as an ongoing process and interpreted judiciously, makes an important contribution to the overall assessment of a child's developmental status.

Test Your Knowledge

REVIEW QUESTIONS

1. List three concerns that may prevent parents from seeking help for their child.

   a.

   b.

   c.

2. List three aspects of early development that can make it difficult to pinpoint a possible problem.

   a.

   b.

   c.

3. List three types of observations that give information about a child's development.

   a.

   b.

   c.

4. List three characteristics of tests appropriate for screening young children.

   a.

   b.

   c.

5. List three reasons why the results of screening tests should be interpreted with caution.

   a.

   b.

   c.

TRUE OR FALSE

1. Reliable screening programs for children from birth through age eight are not readily available.

2. It is always easy to tell the normally developing child from the child who is developing atypically.

3. Developmental problems always show up at birth or within the first few weeks of life.

4. Parents' observations of the child are of little value.

5. The results of screening tests do not predict academic success.

6. A single IQ score is sufficient to determine a child's intellectual capacity both now and in the future.

7. Mother's highest grade level is a fairly safe predictor of her child's success in school.

8. Screening tests measure a child's ability only at the time of testing.

9. Achievement test scores are often expressed in percentile ratings.

10. The economic status of a family seldom influences a child's performance on screening tests.

MULTIPLE CHOICE   *Select one or more correct answers from the lists below.*

1. Parents who fear something is wrong with their child

   a. can be depended on to seek help immediately.

   b. may be uncertain about how to go about getting help.

   c. may not seek further help because a professional told them to stop worrying, that the child will "outgrow" it.

2. It may be difficult even for professionals to identify developmental problems because

   a. a child with a problem may be quite normal in many ways.

   b. a child may have learned to compensate for a development problem (learned to work around it).

   c. the child cannot talk and tell the professional what is wrong.

3. In evaluating the young child, firsthand observation is important because

   a. observation reveals what the child can actually do under everyday conditions.

   b. observations confirm or rule out suspicious or casual impressions about the child.

   c. a child may show skills during a classroom observation not exhibited during a formal testing situation.

4. Screening tests are designed to

   a. predict a child's future academic success.

   b. determine which children need special help.

   c. dictate specific skills to teach a child.

5. The results of screening tests

   a. may indicate the need for further evaluation.

   b. are sufficient evidence for labeling a child as hyperactive.

   c. may lead to a false positive or false negative interpretation.

6. Test scores

   a. always provide accurate assessment of the child's abilities and should never be questioned by parents or caregivers.

   b. often reflect how the child is feeling on a given day, rather than his or her best performance.

   c. are sufficient for formulating a complete diagnosis and treatment guide for children with developmental problems.

CHAPTER 9

WHERE TO SEEK HELP

When the results of screening tests, assessments, or other forms of evaluation indicate the possibility of a developmental delay, prompt referral and early intervention are necessary. Appropriate intervention services may help minimize the effect of delays on other areas of development and improve children's chances of reaching their potential. However, parents, especially those who do not have a family services coordinator, may find themselves bewildered and overwhelmed by the complexity of professional jargon and systems of various service providers. As a result, some parents may do nothing, thus delaying valuable intervention opportunities for their child. When families are provided with sound explanations and assistance in locating appropriate programs and services, such pitfalls can be avoided. Thus, a child is best served when families, teachers, health care professionals, and other members of the developmental team are familiar with parents' rights and the wealth of programs and resources that are available.

LEGISLATION AND PUBLIC POLICY

Several historical pieces of legislation have influenced policy on behalf of infants and young children during the past three decades. Each has been designed to reduce developmental problems through prevention, early identification, and appropriate intervention programs. Not only have these laws assured children and families of specific rights, they also have influenced public attitude. These laws include:

- **P.L. 88-452** (1965). A reflection of the 1960s antipoverty reform, this law provided for the establishment of Head Start and its supplemental services, including developmental screening, medical and dental care, nutritious meals, parent training, and early education for three- and four-year-olds living at or below the poverty level. The educational and developmental benefits for disadvantaged children have been documented by recent studies and thus have contributed to continued increases in federal funding over the years. Amendments to the law in 1972 and 1974 opened Head Start programs to children with disabilities.

- **Early and Periodic Screening, Diagnosis, and Treatment Program (EPSDT)** (1967). This national program was added to Medicaid and designed to locate and evaluate children at developmental risk for medical and psychological problems, and to also address family needs.

- **Supplemental Feeding Program for Women, Infants, and Children (WIC)** (1972). This act created a program aimed at improving maternal health during pregnancy, promoting full-term fetal development, and increasing the birth weight of newborns. Medical supervision, food vouchers, and nutrition education are provided to low-income pregnant women and their children up to the age of five.

- **P.L. 94-142** (1975). Originally called the **Education for All Handicapped Children Act (EHA),** this law was renamed the **Individuals with Disabilities Education Act (IDEA)** (P.L. 101-476) in 1990. A major intent of the act was to motivate states, through financial incentives, to provide comprehensive prevention, treatment, and Individualized Educational Plans (IEPs) for children three to five years old with, and at-risk for developmental problems. (States could choose not to mandate these services.)

- **P.L. 99-547 Education of the Handicapped Act Amendments** (1986). These amendments to P.L. 94-142 are particularly noteworthy because they required states to provide comprehensive special education services to children with developmental disabilities and delays and to include their families through the Individualized Family Service Plan (IFSP). Currently, all states provide free and appropriate educational programs to all three- to five-year-olds. The acts also extended intervention programs to infants and toddlers (Part H); this portion of the bill is not mandatory and, therefore, not all states offer these services. Participating states each determine their own eligibility criteria for conditions that qualify as developmental delays. Additional features of this bill include an emphasis on multidisciplinary assessment, a designated service coordinator, a family-focused approach to a child's problems, and a system of service coordination.

- **P.L. 101-336 Americans with Disabilities Act (ADA)** (1990). This national civil rights law protects against discrimination on the basis of a person's disability. The major intent is to remove barriers that interfere with full inclusion in every aspect of society—education, employment, and public services. Implications for children and their families are clear; by law, child care programs must adapt their settings and programs to accommodate children with disabilities.

THE DEVELOPMENTAL TEAM

Legislative enactments, research findings, and changes in public awareness have significantly altered current educational practices, policies, and program availability for children with developmental delays and disabilities. Best practice suggests that an effective approach to such problems requires a pooling of knowledge and multidisciplinary expertise—in other words, a team approach. Information gathered through a series of interviews, observations, and comprehensive developmental screening provides the most accurate picture of how a delay in one area affects development in other areas, just as progress in one area supports progress in others. For example, a two-year-old with a moderate hearing loss could experience delays in language, cognitive, and social development. Thus, appropriate intervention strategies for this child may require the input and services of an audiologist, speech and language therapist, early childhood teacher, nurse, and, perhaps, a social service agency. However, if a team approach is to benefit the child's overall development, effective communication and cooperation among specialists, service providers, and the family is essential.

Federal law requires that parents be involved in all phases of the assessment and intervention process. Parents, working in collaboration with professionals, become important members of the child's developmental team. A family-centered approach improves the sharing of valuable information, and enables parents to learn and implement therapy recommendations at home. Sustained interest and participation in their child's intervention program can be achieved if the developmental team:

- keeps parents informed
- explains rationales for treatment procedures
- emphasizes the child's progress
- teaches parents how to work with their child at home
- provides parents with positive feedback for their continued efforts and advocacy on the child's behalf

Identifying the problem.

REFERRALS

The referral process involves a multiple-step approach. Initially, the child's strengths, weaknesses, and developmental skills are evaluated by an assessment team. The family's needs and resources (e.g., financial, psychological, physical, transportation) available to care for the child must also be taken into consideration. For example, if a family cannot afford special services, has no knowledge of financial assistance programs, and does not own a car, it is unlikely that they will carry out recommendations for professional treatment. However, rarely are such problems insurmountable. Most communities have individuals and social service agencies available to help families locate and utilize needed services.

When child and family needs and priorities have been identified, an intervention program can be planned. Depending on the nature of the developmental delay, a child may be eligible to receive special services. An Individual Family Service Plan (IFSP—for infants and toddlers) or Individualized Educational Plan (IEP—for preschool through school age) is written to address the child's individual needs. A family service coordinator works closely with the family, matching their needs with service agencies and educational programs in the community. The service coordinator also assists the family in establishing initial contacts and making final arrangements.

For many families, the process of approaching multiple agencies and dealing with bureaucratic red tape is overwhelming. As a result, these families often do not, or cannot, complete the necessary arrangements unless they receive assistance and on-going support. The role of a service coordinator is so crucial to successful intervention that it has been written into federal legislation (P.L. 99-457) to help families and young children with developmental disabilities.

Placement in an early childhood educational setting is frequently recommended as part of the child's intervention plan. In these settings, classroom teachers and other members of the developmental team conduct ongoing assessments of the child's progress. In addition, the developmental team also reviews the appropriateness of placements and special services on a regular basis to determine if the child's and family's needs are being met. This step is especially critical with infants and toddlers, whose developmental needs change quickly. Throughout, there must be continuing communication and support among teachers, practitioners, and parents to ensure that the intervention program is of maximum benefit to the child.

RESOURCES

Many resources are available to families, teachers, and service providers who work with young children. These resources are provided at the community, state, and national levels and fall into two major categories: direct services and information sources.

Direct Services

Numerous agencies and organizations provide developmental screenings and direct services to children with developmental delays and their families. Many also provide technical assistance to educators and professionals who work with these children. In addition, agencies themselves often serve as valuable referral sources because they are familiar with other community-based services, programs, and qualified specialists, including:

- Child Find screening programs
- Interagency Coordinating Councils (ICCs)
- Early childhood centers and therapeutic programs for exceptional children
- Public health departments at city, county, and state levels
- Local public school districts, especially the special services divisions
- Hospitals, medical centers, and well-child clinics
- University-Affiliated Programs (UAPs)
- Head Start and Even Start programs
- Mental health centers
- Professional practitioners: pediatricians, nurses, psychologists, audiologists, ophthalmologists, early childhood specialists, educators, speech-language therapists, occupational and physical therapists, and social workers

Most communities also offer a variety of services and agencies designed to help families cope with the special challenges and demands of caring for a child with developmental disabilities. A child's developmental problems affect every family member and often cause stress and inescapable adjustments in family lifestyles. However, many emotional and financial problems can be eased or avoided altogether if the family receives early assistance and support in the form of marriage counseling, financial management, mental health counseling, medical care, or help with transportation, housekeeping, or child care.

Direct assistance may also be provided through the efforts of local service groups. These organizations are familiar with community needs and often provide specific and important types of assistance, including financial donations, transportation, **respite care,** and assistance with the purchase of special equipment.

Parent support groups represent yet another direct service-oriented resource. These community groups provide opportunities for families to share their daily experiences with other families having similar problems and concerns. In addition, parents can be supported and encouraged as they work to strengthen their own parenting skills, learning effective behavior management for children with special needs.

---

respite care—Child care assistance given to families to allow them temporary relief from the demands of caring for a disabled child.

**Services for children with developmental
problems are available from a variety
of agencies.**

A number of national organizations also provide direct assistance to children and families with specific needs. Their addresses can be located in most telephone directories or the *Encyclopedia of Associations* found at public libraries. Many of these organizations also maintain Web sites for improved access, including:

- Down Syndrome Children (*www.downsnet.org*)
- The American Foundation for the Blind (*www.afb.org*)
- Learning Disabilities Association (*www.ldanatl.org*)
- The United States Cerebral Palsy Athletic Association (*www.uscpaa.org*)
- The Autism Society of America (*www.autism-society.org*)
- American Speech, Language, Hearing Association (ASHA) (*www.asha.org*)
- Epilepsy Foundation of America (*www.efa.org*)
- National Easter Seals (*www.easter-seals.org*)

There are also a number of programs and organizations whose purpose is to provide direct, technical assistance to educational programs and agencies serving young children with developmental disabilities. Many of these groups also offer instructional material. A sample of such agencies includes:

- National Information Center for Children and Youth with Disabilities.
- Head Start Resource Access Projects (RAPs). Their purpose is to assist Head Start programs in providing comprehensive services to children with developmental problems.
- National Early Childhood-Technical Assistance System (NEC-TAS). This agency provides many types of assistance to federally funded projects for children with disabilities.

- American Printing House for the Blind. This group produces materials and services for children with visual impairments, including talking books, magazines in braille, and large-type books, as well as materials intended for educators of blind or visually impaired children.

Information Sources

A wealth of information is published for parents, caregivers, and professionals who work with children with developmental problems. Many professional journals, government publications, CD-ROMS, and reference books are available in most public and university libraries. Special interest groups and professional organizations also produce a wealth of printed materials focused on high-risk children and children with developmental delays. Only a few are listed here:

- Professional journals and periodicals, such as the *Journal of the Division for Early Childhood, Topics in Early Childhood Special Education, Exceptional Children*, and *Teaching Exceptional Children.*
- Trade magazines for parents, such as *Parents of Exceptional Children, Parenting,* and *Parents Magazine.*
- Government documents, reports, and pamphlets. These cover almost any topic related to child development, child care, early intervention, nutrition, parenting, and specific developmental problems. Publications can be obtained through the Superintendent of Documents, U.S. Government Printing Office, Washington, DC 20402; many are available in local government buildings, including public libraries and on the Internet.
- Bibliographic indexes and abstracts usually located in university, college, and large public libraries. These are particularly useful to students and practitioners who need to locate information quickly on a specific topic. Two of many examples include:
  - *The Review of Child Development*
  - *Current Topics in Early Childhood Education*

- Professional associations that focus on children's issues include:
  - Council for Exceptional Children (CEC), especially the Division for Early Childhood (DEC) within the Council (*www.cec.sped.org*)
  - National Association for the Education of Young Children (NAEYC) (*www.naeyc.org./naeyc*)
  - Association for Retarded Citizens (ARC) (*www.thearc.org*)
  - American Association on Mental Retardation (AAMR) (*www.aamr.org*)
  - Children's Defense Fund (*www.childrensdefense.org*)
  - American Speech, Language, Hearing Association (ASHA) (*www.asha.org*)

- National Parent Information Network (NPIN) (*http://ericps.ed.uiuc.edu/npin/npinhome.html*)
- American Academy of Pediatrics (*www.aap.org*)
- American Public Health Association (*www.apha.org*)
- The National Information Center for Children and Youth with Disabilities (*www.nichcy.org*)

In conclusion, finding help for children with developmental delays and disabilities is not a simple matter. The issues are often complex—some children present tangles of interrelated developmental problems that tend to multiply when not addressed during the crucial first five years of life. Therefore, effective intervention must begin early, be comprehensive, integrated, and ongoing. It must take into account multiple developmental areas at the same time. This effort requires teamwork on the part of specialists from many disciplines, service providers, and agencies working cooperatively with the child and the family. It also requires an awareness of legislative acts and public policies that affect services for children with developmental problems and their families, as well as available resources and effective means of collaboration. Only then will children and families fully benefit from an early intervention team approach.

Test Your Knowledge

REVIEW QUESTIONS

1. List three professional providers who typically serve on a developmental team.

   a.

   b.

   c.

2. List three methods that a developmental team can use to foster family involvement.

   a.

   b.

   c.

3. List three sources where intervention services are available for a child and family with developmental problems.

   a.

   b.

   c.

4. List three organizations that focus solely on specific developmental disabilities.

   a.

   b.

   c.

5. List three pieces of federal legislation enacted since 1970 that serve young children who are at-risk for, or have, a disabling condition.

   a.

   b.

   c.

TRUE OR FALSE

1. Parents rarely have difficulty arranging for intervention services, especially when they care about their child.

2. A delay in one developmental area almost always affects progress in other developmental areas.

3. A parent with limited income probably cannot afford most intervention programs and services for a disabled child.

4. Family service coordinators are an unnecessary expenditure, even a luxury, on most developmental teams.

5. Suitable publications for use by parents and teachers are available from government agencies.

6. WIC is a federal program aimed at helping unemployed mothers learn a job skill.

7. Effective intervention must be concerned with all areas of development simultaneously.

8. Child Find programs are designed to locate missing and abused children.

9. Placement in early childhood programs is frequently recommended by developmental teams.

10. Until professionals have completed their assessments, parents should play only a limited role in the screening and intervention process.

MULTIPLE CHOICE   *Select one or more correct answers from the lists below.*

1. A young child who has an undetected hearing loss may have problems with

    a. language

    b. social development

    c. cognitive development

2. Organizations providing assistance to disabled children and their families include

    a. Autism Society of America

    b. Audubon Society

    c. American Foundation for the Blind

3. The role of a family service coordinator is to

    a. assist parents through the team process

    b. keep parents informed of each step the team takes on behalf of the child

    c. reprimand parents when they fail to keep records or appointments with team members

4. The referral process includes

    a. identification of a child's problems

    b. decisions as to which professionals would best serve the child's needs

    c. helping locate transportation for families unable to provide it themselves

5. P.L.99-457 mandates

    a. an individual service plan (ISP) for the entire family

    b. federal money for setting up early identification and intervention programs within each state

    c. stiff fines for parents or teachers who fail to report a disabling condition to proper authorities

APPENDIX

SUMMARY OF REFLEXES

Age	Appears	Disappears
Birth	swallow*, gag*, cough*, yawn*, blink, suck, rooting, Moro (startle), grasp, stepping, plantar, elimination, Tonic neck reflex (TNR)	
1–4 months	Landau, tear* (cries with tears)	grasp, suck (becomes voluntary), step, root, Tonic neck reflex (TNR), Moro (startle)
4–8 months	parachute, palmar grasp, pincer grasp	
8–12 months		palmar grasp, plantar reflex
12–18 months		
18–24 months		Landau, parachute, elimination (becomes voluntary)
3–4 years		

*Permanent; present throughout person's lifetime.

APPENDIX 2

DEVELOPMENTAL CHECKLISTS

A simple checklist, one for each child, is a useful observation tool for anyone working with infants and young children. Questions on the checklists that follow can be answered during the course of a child's everyday activities and over a period of a week or more. "No" answers signal further investigation may be in order. Several "no" answers indicate that additional investigation is a necessity.

The "sometimes" category is an important one. It suggests what the child can do, at least part of the time, or under some circumstances. The "sometimes" category provides space where brief notes and comments can be recorded about how and when a behavior occurs. In many cases, a child may simply need more practice, incentive, or adult encouragement. Hunches often provide a good starting point for working with the child. Again, if "sometimes" is checked a number of times, further investigation is recommended.

The observation checklists may be duplicated and used as part of the assessment process. A completed checklist contains information about a child that members of a developmental team would find useful in evaluating a child's development status and in determining an intervention program.

Child's Name _____ Age _____

Observer _____ Date _____

DEVELOPMENTAL CHECKLIST

BY TWELVE MONTHS:
Does the child . . .
Walk with assistance?
Roll a ball in imitation of an adult?
Pick objects up with thumb and forefinger?
Transfer objects from one hand to other hand?
Pick up dropped toys?
Look directly at adult's face?
Imitate gestures: peek-a-boo, bye-bye,
   pat-a-cake?
Find object hidden under a cup?
Feed self crackers (munching, not sucking
   on them)?
Hold cup with two hands; drink with
   assistance?
Smile spontaneously?
Pay attention to own name?
Respond to "no"?
Respond differently to strangers and
   familiar persons?
Respond differently to sounds: vacuum,
   phone, door?
Look at person who speaks to him or her?
Respond to simple directions accompanied
   by gestures?
Make several consonant–vowel combination
   sounds?
Vocalize back to person who has talked to
   him or her?
Use intonation patterns that sound like
   scolding, asking, exclaiming?
Say "da-da" or "ma-ma"?
	Yes	No	Sometimes

Child's Name _____   Age _____

Observer _____   Date _____

DEVELOPMENTAL CHECKLIST

BY TWO YEARS:	Yes	No	Sometimes
Does the child . . .			
Walk alone?			
Bend over and pick up toy without falling over?			
Seat self in child-size chair? Walk up and down stairs with assistance?			
Place several rings on a stick?			
Place five pegs in a pegboard?			
Turn pages two or three at a time?			
Scribble?			
Follow one-step direction involving something familiar: "Give me—." "Show me—." "Get a—."?			
Match familiar objects?			
Use spoon with some spilling?			
Drink from cup holding it with one hand, unassisted?			
Chew food?			
Take off coat, shoe, sock?			
Zip and unzip large zipper?			
Recognize self in mirror or picture?			
Refer to self by name?			
Imitate adult behaviors in play—for example, feeds "baby"?			
Help put things away?			
Respond to specific words by showing what was named: toy, pet, family member?			
Ask for desired items by name: (cookie)?			
Answer with name of object when asked "What's that"?			
Make some two-word statements: "Daddy bye-bye"?			

Child's Name _____   Age _____

Observer _____   Date _____

DEVELOPMENTAL CHECKLIST

BY THREE YEARS: Does the child . . .	Yes	No	Sometimes
Run well in a forward direction?			
Jump in place, two feet together?			
Walk on tiptoe?			
Throw ball (but without direction or aim)? Kick ball forward?			
String four large beads?			
Turn pages in book singly?			
Hold crayon: imitate circular, vertical, horizontal strokes?			
Match shapes?			

Demonstrate number concepts of one and
    two? (Can select one or two; can tell if one or
    two objects.)			

Use spoon without spilling?			
Drink from a straw?			
Put on and take off coat?			
Wash and dry hands with some assistance?			
Watch other children; play near them; some- times join in their play?			
Defend own possessions?			

Use symbols in play—for example, tin pan on
    head becomes helmet and crate becomes a
    space ship?			

Respond to "Put _____ in the box," "Take the _____ out of the box"?			
Select correct item on request: big vs. little; one vs. two?			

Identify objects by their use: show own shoe
    when asked, "What do you wear on
    your feet?"			

Ask questions?			

Tell about something with functional phrases
    that carry meaning: "Daddy go airplane."
    "Me hungry now"?			

Child's Name _____   Age _____

Observer _____   Date _____

DEVELOPMENTAL CHECKLIST

BY FOUR YEARS: Does the child . . . Walk on a line? Balance on one foot briefly? Hop on one foot? Jump over an object 6 inches high and land on both feet together? Throw ball with direction? Copy circles and crosses? Match six colors? Count to 5? Pour well from pitcher? Spread butter, jam with knife? Button, unbutton large buttons? Know own sex, age, last name? Use toilet independently and reliably? Wash and dry hands unassisted? Listen to stories for at least 5 minutes? Draw head of person and at least one other body part? Play with other children? Share, take turns (with some assistance)? Engage in dramatic and pretend play? Respond appropriately to "Put it beside," "Put it under"? Respond to two-step directions: "Give me the sweater and put the shoe on the floor"? Respond by selecting the correct object—for example, hard vs. soft object? Answer 'if," "what," and "when" questions? Answer questions about function: "What are books for"?	Yes	No	Sometimes

Child's Name _____ Age _____

Observer _____ Date _____

DEVELOPMENTAL CHECKLIST

BY FIVE YEARS: Does the child . . . Walk backward, heel to toe? Walk up and down stairs, alternating feet? Cut on line? Print some letters? Point to and name three shapes? Group common related objects: shoe, sock, and foot: apple, orange, and plum? Demonstrate number concepts to 4 or 5? Cut food with a knife: celery, sandwich? Lace shoes? Read from story picture book—in other words, tell story by looking at pictures? Draw a person with three to six body parts? Play and interact with other children; engage in dramatic play that is close to reality? Build complex structures with blocks or other building materials? Respond to simple three-step directions: "Give me the pencil, put the book on the table, and hold the comb in your hand"? Respond correctly when asked to show penny, nickel, and dime? Ask "How" questions? Respond verbally to "Hi" and "How are you"? Tell about event using past and future tenses? Use conjunctions to string words and phrases together—for example, "I saw a bear and a zebra and a giraffe at the zoo"?	Yes	No	Sometimes

Child's Name _____   Age _____

Observer _____   Date _____

DEVELOPMENTAL CHECKLIST

BY SIX YEARS: Does the child . . .	Yes	No	Sometimes
Walk across a balance beam?			
Skip with alternating feet?			
Hop for several seconds on one foot?			
Cut out simple shapes?			
Copy own first name?			
Show well-established handedness; demonstrate consistent right or left handedness?			
Sort objects on one or more dimensions: color, shape, or function?			
Name most letters and numerals?			
Count by rote to 10; know what number comes next?			
Dress self completely; tie bows?			
Brush teeth unassisted?			
Have some concept of clock time in relation to daily schedule?			
Cross street safely?			
Draw a person with head, trunk, legs, arms, and features; often add clothing details?			
Play simple board games?			
Engage in cooperative play with other children, involving group decisions, role assignments, rule observance?			
Use construction toys, such as Leggos, blocks, to make recognizable structures?			
Do fifteen piece puzzles?			
Use all grammatical structures: pronouns, plurals, verb tenses, conjunctions?			
Use complex sentences: carry on conversations?			

Child's Name _____   Age _____

Observer _____   Date _____

DEVELOPMENTAL CHECKLIST

BY SEVEN YEARS: Does the child . . . Concentrate on completing puzzles and board games? Ask many questions? Use correct verb tenses, word order, and sentence structure in conversation? Correctly identify right and left hands? Make friends easily? Show some control of anger, using words instead of physical aggression? Participate in play that requires teamwork and rule observance? Seek adult approval for efforts? Enjoy reading and being read to? Use pencil to write words and numbers? Sleep undisturbed through the night? Catch a tennis ball, walk across balance beam, hit ball with bat? Plan and carry out simple projects with minimal adult help? Tie own shoes? Draw pictures with greater detail and sense of proportion? Care for own personal needs with some adult supervision? Wash hands? Brush teeth? Use toilet? Dress self? Show some understanding of cause-and-effect concepts?	Yes	No	Sometimes

Child's Name _____ Age _____

Observer _____ Date _____

DEVELOPMENTAL CHECKLIST

BY EIGHT AND NINE YEARS: Does the child . . .	Yes	No	Sometimes
Have energy to play, continuing growth, few illnesses?			
Use pencil in a deliberate and controlled manner?			
Express relatively complex thoughts in a clear and logical fashion?			
Carry out multiple (4–5)-step instructions?			
Become less easily frustrated with own performance?			
Interact and play cooperatively with other children?			
Show interest in creative expression—telling stories, jokes, writing, drawing, singing?			
Use eating utensils with ease?			
Have a good appetite? Show interest in trying new foods?			
Know how to tell time?			
Have control of bowel and bladder functions?			
Participate in some group activities—games, sports, plays?			
Want to go to school? Seem disappointed if must miss a day?			
Demonstrate beginning skills in reading, writing, and math?			
Accept responsibility and complete work independently?			
Handle stressful situations without becoming overly upset?			

APPENDIX 3

CHILD HEALTH HISTORY

SAMPLE FORM

We appreciate your taking time to fill out this form as completely as possible. The information will be treated in a confidential manner and used for evaluating and for planning your child's program.

GENERAL INFORMATION

1. Child's Name _____   _____
   (First)   (Last)

2. Child's Address   _____
   (Street)

   _____
   (City, State, Zip)

3. Home Telephone Number __(___)_____

4. Child's Gender: _____ Female _____ Male

5. Child's Date of Birth   _____   _____   _____
   Month   Date   Year

6. Mother's Name _____

7. Father's Name _____

BIRTH HISTORY

8. Length of Pregnancy: ___ 6 ___ 7 ___ 8 ___ 9 months

9. Child's weight at birth: ___lbs. ___ozs. or ___ kilograms

10. Were there any unusual factors or complications during this pregnancy? ___ yes ___ no. Please describe: _____

11. Did your child have any medical problems at birth? i.e., jaundice, difficulty breathing, birth defects ___ yes ___ no. Please describe: _____

_____

12. Which doctor is most familiar with your child? _____

    doctor's telephone number: (___)_____

13. Does your child take any medications on a regular basis? ___ yes ___ no. If yes, name of medication and dosage: _____

14. Has your child had any of the following illnesses (dates)?

    ___ measles   ___ rheumatic fever

    ___ mumps   ___ chicken pox

    ___ whooping cough   ___ pneumonia

    ___ middle ear infection   ___ hepatitis
        (otitis media)

    ___ meningitis

15. Where there any complications with these illnesses, such as high fever, convulsions, muscle weaknesses, and so on? ___ yes ___ no. Please describe:

_____

16. Has your child ever been hospitalized? ___ yes ___ no. Number of times ___ Total length of time _____

    Reasons: _____

17. Has your child had any other serious illness or injuries that did not involve hospitalization? ___ yes ___ no

    Please describe: _____

18. How many colds has your child had during the past year? _____

19. Does your child have:

    Allergies? ___ yes ___ no. (please specify which allergies):

    Foods _____

    Animals _____

    Medicine _____

Asthma? ___ yes ___ no

Hayfever? ___ yes ___ no

20. Has your child had any problems with earaches or ear infections? ___ yes ___ no
If yes, how often in the past year?_____

21. Has your child's hearing been tested? ___ yes ___ no

Date of test: _____ _____ Was there any evidence of hearing loss? __ yes __ no
                (month)   (year)

If yes, describe: _____

22. Does your child currently have tubes in his or her ears? ___ yes ___ no

23. Do you have any concerns about your child's speech or language development?
___ yes ___ no. If yes, describe: _____

24. Has your child's vision been tested? ___ yes ___ no

Date of test: _____ _____
            (month)   (year)

25. Was there any evidence of vision loss? ___ yes ___ no

Please describe: _____

26. Does your child do some things that you find troublesome?

Please describe: _____

27. Has your child ever participated in out-of-the-home child care services—for
example, sitter, day care, preschool? ___ yes ___ no. Please describe: _____

_____

CHILD'S PLAY ACTIVITIES

28. Where does your child usually play—for example, backyard, kitchen, bedroom?

_____

29. Does your child usually play: ___ alone? ___ with one to two other children?
___ with brothers/sisters?

___ with older children?   ___ with younger children?

___ with children of the same age?

30. Is your child usually ___ cooperative? ___ shy? ___ aggressive?

31. What are some of your child's favorite toys and activities?

    Please describe: _____

32. Are there any particular behaviors you would like us to watch?

    Please describe: _____

    _____

CHILD'S DAILY ROUTINE

33. Do you have any concerns about your child's:

    ___ eating habits?

    ___ sleeping habits?

    ___ toilet training?

    If yes, please describe: _____

34. Is your child toilet trained? ___ yes ___ no. If yes, how often does your child have an accident? _____

35. What word(s) does your child use or understand for:

    urination _____ bowel movement _____

36. How many hours does your child sleep? At night _____ ?

    Goes to bed at: ___ P.M. Wakes up at: ___ A.M.   Afternoon nap: _____

37. When your child is upset, how do you comfort him or her? _____

    _____

38. The term *family* has many different meanings. Since the topic of families and family members is often included in classroom discussions, please list or describe who your child considers to be "family" at home. _____

    _____

39. How many brothers and (or) sisters does your child have?
    Brothers (ages): _____ Sisters (ages): _____

    _____ _____

    _____ _____

40. What language(s) is/(are) most commonly spoken in your home?
    English _____ Other _____

41. Is there any additional information that would help us understand or work more effectively with your child? _____

    _____

APPENDIX 4

ASSESSMENT INSTRUMENTS

EXAMPLES OF SCREENING TESTS

AGS Early Screening Profiles test children two to seven years of age for cognitive, language, social, self-help, and motor skills; includes information provided by parents, teachers, and child care providers.

Denver Developmental Screening Test (Denver II) is appropriate for testing children from birth to six years of age in four developmental areas: personal/social, language, fine motor, and gross motor. Ratings of the child's behavior during testing can be recorded.

Developmental Activities Screening Inventory (DASI II) screens children one month to five years; a nonverbal test especially useful for children with hearing or language disorders; also offers adaptations for children with vision problems.

Developmental Indicators for the Assessment of Learning—Revised (DIAL-R) is designed to screen children two years to five years, nine months, in motor, concept, and language development; includes a checklist of social-emotional behaviors observed during testing. A Parent Information Form related to child's health and home–school experiences is part of the kit.

First Steps: Screening Test for Evaluating Preschoolers can be used with children two years, nine months, to six years, two months, on cognitive, communication, and motor skills; an Adaptive Behavior Checklist and a Social-Emotional Scale is included as well as a Parent–Teacher Scale related to the child's behavior at home and at school.

EXAMPLES OF ASSESSMENT INSTRUMENTS

APGAR Scoring System is administered at one minute and again at five minutes after birth; the APGAR assesses muscle tone, respiration, color, heart beat, and reflexes for a maximum score of 10. The information is used to determine which infants need special care.

Neonatal Behavioral Assessment Scale (NBAS—often referred to as *The Brazelton*) assesses behavioral responses in full-term infants up to twenty-eight days of age. A significant modification of the NBAS is the *Kansas Supplement (NBAS-K)*. It adds a number of critical parameters and also assesses the infant's typical behavior (state) as well as optimal behavior (the only focus of the original NBAS).

Kaufman Assessment Battery for Children is used with children from two-and-one-half to twelve years of age to test children's mental processing abilities. The test items are designed to minimize the effects of verbal, gender, and ethnic bias.

Learning Accomplishment Profile—Diagnostic Standardized Assessment (LAP-D) assesses children two-and-one-half through age six on fine motor (writing and manipulative skills), gross motor (such as body and object movement), matching and counting (viewed as cognitive tasks), and language skills (comprehension and object naming).

Bayley Scales of Infant Development evaluate both motor and cognitive development. The age range has been expanded to cover children from one month to three-and-one-half years. The Mental Scales and the Motor Scales are separate instruments.

Peabody Developmental Motor Scales evaluate children from birth through seven years of age in fine motor (grasping, eye–hand coordination, and manual dexterity) and gross motor development (reflexes, balance, locomotion, throwing, and catching).

Kaufman Survey of Early Academic and Language Skills assesses three- to six-year-olds' reception and expressive language skills as well as concepts related to numbers, counting, letters, and words; includes an articulation survey.

Peabody Picture Vocabulary Test—Revised can be used with children age three into adulthood; it is a test of receptive language with an adaptation for individuals with motor impairments; a Spanish-language version is available.

Preschool Language Scale assesses children one to three years of age on auditory comprehension, articulation, grammatical forms, and basic concept development.

Early Childhood Environment Rating Scale (ECERS) provides a comprehensive assessment of the classroom environment: space, materials, activities, supervision, child–child and adult–child interactions. Useful in infant, toddler, and preschool settings.

Home Observation for Measurement of the Environment (HOME) is the best known and most widely used of in-home inventories. Scales range from infancy to middle childhood; each version assesses the physical environment as well as the social, emotional, and cognitive support available to the child.

Audiology, that is, hearing assessment of infants and children requires clinical testing by a trained technician. It is *imperative,* however, in terms of early identification, that teachers and parents record and report their observations whenever they suspect a child is not hearing well. Warning signs include:

- pulling or banging on an ear;
- drainage from ear canal;
- failing to respond or looking puzzled when spoken to;
- requesting frequent repetitions—What? Huh?;
- speaking in too loud or too soft of a voice;
- articulating or discriminating sounds poorly.

The Snellen E or *Illiterate E* test is an instrument commonly used for assessing the visual acuity of young children (knowing the alphabet is not required). As with hearing, screening of young children for vision problems relies heavily on parents' and teachers' informal observations and telltale signs such as:

- rubbing eyes frequently or closing or covering one eye;
- constantly stumbling over, or running into, things;
- complaining of frequent headaches;
- blinking excessively when looking at books or reading;
- brushing hand over eyes as if trying to get rid of a blur.

APPENDIX 5

ANNOTATED BIBLIOGRAPHY AND REFERENCES

CHILD DEVELOPMENT

Bee, H. (1998). *The developing child* (8th ed.). New York: HarperCollins.
This comprehensive child development text is highly readable. It provides a psychologically sound, yet conversational, coverage of all aspects of child development. Throughout, research findings are reported in such a way that they are readily related to everyday home and school settings.

Berk, L. A. (1997). *Child development* (4th ed.). Boston, MA: Allyn & Bacon.
The fundamentals of child development are presented in a clear and chronological manner. Many contemporary topics are addressed, with special emphasis on the influence of culture on children's development, the application of research to practice, and social policy as it affects children and families.

Berns, R. (1994). *Topical child development*. Albany, NY: Delmar Publishers.
Written by a sensitive child developmentalist, this text combines psychological theory and research in ways that are delightfully descriptive and readily applicable to the lives of children (a topical approach).

Bjorklund, D., and Bjorklund, B. (1992). *Looking at children*. Pacific Groves, CA: Brooks/Cole Publishing Company.
An introductory text for practitioners that skillfully blends theory and research with practical application in language that is clear and understandable.

Charlesworth, R. (1996) (4th ed.). *Understanding child development*. Albany, NY: Delmar Publishers.
An excellent book for teachers, caregivers, and parents; the focus is on growth and development in the infant, toddler, and preschool child. A wealth of basic information is skillfully combined with numerous suggestions for working with young children.

Cole, M., and Cole, S. (1993). *The development of children*. New York: Scientific American Books.
This child development text presents the fundamental theories and contemporary issues,

inclusive of birth through adolescence, in a thorough and readable style with a strong emphasis on the influence of culture.

Flavell, J. H. (1992). *Cognitive development.* Englewood Cliffs, NJ: Prentice-Hall.
No text on cognitive development can completely escape technical complexity, but this one, written by a leading researcher on cognitive development and developmental theory, is one of the best, yet least difficult, because of its easy, anecdotal style.

Fogel, A. (1997). *Infancy.* New York: West Publishing Company.
A comprehensive overview of child development, conception through age three, which examines a number of contemporary factors that influence individual differences, including intelligence, sociability, and temperament.

Kopp, C. (1993). *Baby steps: The "why's" of your child's behavior in the first two years.* New York: W. H. Freeman Company.
Based on contemporary research, this book provides a step-by-step description of infant and toddler development in the social, cognitive, emotional, motor, and perceptual domains.

Santrock, J. W. (1997). *Children* (5th ed.). Dubuque, IA: Wm. C. Brown Publishers.
An appealing and easily read textbook that addresses contemporary topics in child development in a culturally sensitive manner. Extensive research findings, with emphasis on everyday application, are incorporated throughout the book.

OBSERVATION AND ASSESSMENT

Bentzen, M. (1997). *Seeing young children: A guide to observing and recording behavior* (3rd ed.). Albany, NY: Delmar Publishers.
A practical book on observing young children, recording their developmental progress, and using the information to foster each child's development in multiple areas.

Hills, T. W. (1992). Reaching potentials through appropriate assessment. In S. Bradekamp and T. Rosegrant (Eds.), *Reaching potentials: Appropriate curriculum and assessment for young children* (vol. 1, pp. 43–63). Washington, DC: National Association for the Education of Young Children.
The entire volume is worthwhile, with this particular essay pointing out how direct observation of children is a major source of information for designing both individual and group curriculum activities.

Irwin, D. M., and Bushnell, M. M. (1980). *Observational strategies for child study.* New York: Rinehart & Winston.
Though not a recent publication, this text is still a classic. It offers detailed instructions and exercises designed to teach all major observation strategies, as well as giving thorough coverage of the history of child observation.

McAfee, O., and Leong, D. (1997). *Assessing and guiding young children's development and learning.* Boston, MA: Allyn & Bacon.
This is an excellent book that covers authentic assessment and screening strategies in easily

understood detail; many examples are also included. The authors stress assessment as a process, sensitivity to individual differences, and professional responsibility.

McLean, M., Bailey, D., and Wolery, M. (1996). *Assessing infants and preschoolers with special needs* (2nd ed.). Columbus, OH: Prentice-Hall.

An excellent book written for early childhood educators and allied health professionals. The authors stress the importance of observation in natural settings, a family-centered approach, and sensitivity to cultural differences.

Mindes, G., Ireton, H., and Mardell-Czudnowski, C. (1996). *Assessing young children.* Albany, NY: Delmar Publishers.

This book provides valuable information about a range of assessment strategies, including a review of screening tools and suppliers. Emphasis is placed on the appropriate use of assessment findings for making sound decisions that affect young children and planning developmentally appropriate practices.

Nilsen, B. A. (1997). *Week by week: Observing and recording young children.* Albany, NY: Delmar Publishers.

The author presents a systematic yet feasible plan for documenting children's behavior. Various methods of observing and recording are featured along with principles of child development and appropriate classroom practices. Teacher trainers, practicum students, and classroom teachers will find this text most useful.

CHILDREN WITH SPECIAL NEEDS

Allen, K. E., and Schwartz, I. (1996). *The exceptional child: Inclusion in early childhood education* (3rd ed.). Albany, NY: Delmar Publishers.

A comprehensive text based on developmental principles as they are applied to the inclusion and appropriate education of children of all developmental capabilities in early childhood programs.

Blackman, J. A. (1997). *Medical aspects of developmental disabilities in children birth through three.* Rockville, MD: Aspen Systems.

A highly recommended book for early childhood personnel; it provides well-illustrated and readily understood information about medical issues that affect the developmental progress of young children.

Hanson, M., and Harris, S. (1986). *Teaching the young child with motor delays.* Austin, TX: Pro-Ed Publishers.

An easy-to-read book bridging the gap between parents and clinicians working with children birth to age three with motor impairments; includes teaching strategies and therapy activities that can be used in the home and child care programs.

Johnson, L. J., Gallagher, R. J., LaMontagne, M. J., Jordan, J. B., Gallagher, J. J., Hutinger, P. L., and Karnes, M. B. (Eds.). (1994). *Meeting early intervention challenges.* Baltimore: Paul H. Brookes.

Written by noted professionals in the field, this book examines key issues and challenges associated with early intervention services for young children and their families. A strong commitment to professional collaboration and a transdisciplinary team approach is evident throughout the book.

McCormick, L., and Schiefelbusch, R. (1994). *Early language intervention.* Columbus, OH: Charles E. Merrill.

An excellent introduction to both normal and atypical language development; includes practical examples of programs, procedures, and materials for enhancing communication skills in young children.

Noonan, M. J., and McCormick, L. (1993). *Early intervention in natural environments.* Pacific Grove, CA: Brooks/Cole Publishing Company.

A superior text that responds to the federal mandate to serve infants and young children with developmental problems in the natural environment of the family's choice, using play and other developmentally appropriate activities and learning opportunities.

Roush, J., and Matkin, N. (Eds.). (1994). *Infants and toddlers with hearing loss: Family-centered assessment and intervention.* Baltimore, MD: York Press.

The authors present valuable information on various hearing disorders in young children and discuss assessment techniques that are appropriate and family-focused.

Swan, W. W., and Morgan, J. L. (1993). *Collaboration for comprehensive services for young children and their families.* Baltimore, MD: Paul Brookes.

A hands-on book that includes useful advice on creating and improving local interagency collaboration systems; examines their role, organizational and procedural concerns, financing, how to facilitate collaboration, and outcome evaluation.

Zipper, I., Weil, M., and Rounds, K. (1996). *Service coordination for early intervention: Parents and professionals.* Cambridge, MA: Brookline Books.

Valuable resource information is provided in this book to help parents and professionals develop early intervention programs with a strong family focus. Many logistical concerns in establishing intervention services are discussed, including provider roles, fostering collaboration, evaluating outcomes, staffing, and developing sensitivity to individual differences.

DIVERSITY

deMelendez, W., and Ostertag, V. (1997). *Teaching young children in multicultural classrooms: Issues, concepts and strategies.* Albany, NY: Delmar Publishers.

The authors describe themselves as "newcomers" to America, but they obviously are not newcomers to the cultural diversity represented in our schools and child care centers. This well-organized text lays out plans for developing a functional, multicultural curriculum. In addition, it provides an insightful perspective on the history as well as the future of multiculturalism in our schools and country.

Gordon, A., and Browne, K. W. (1996). *Guiding young children in a diverse society.* Boston, MA: Allyn & Bacon.

The text is based on the premise that sound developmental principles apply to all children, regardless of their cultural backgrounds. A counterpoint is also examined: that teachers must employ cultural sensitivity when parents challenge the traditional early childhood philosophy. A worthwhile examination of increasingly diverse views of early education.

Isenberg, J. P., and Jalongo, M. R. (Eds.). (1997). *Major issues and trends in early childhood education.* New York: Teachers College Press.
A series of articles in which the authors examine current issues and challenges in the field with respect to public policy, inclusion, diversity, family involvement, DAP, and assessment.

Lynch, E. W., and Hanson, M. J. (1992). *Developing cross-cultural competence: A guide to working with young children and their families.* Baltimore, MD: Paul Brookes.
Cultural, language, and developmental diversity among children and their families is the focus of this well-researched text. Chapters 4–11 offer detailed insights into seven of the most common cultures represented in schools and child care centers today. Cultural differences are described and analyzed by the authors, each native to their respective culture.

McCracken, J. B. (1993). *Valuing diversity: The primary years.* Washington, DC: NAEYC.
A good resource book that highlights the importance of recognizing and implementing practices that embrace individual differences.

PARENTING

A reader's guide for parents of children with mental, physical or emotional disabilities. (1990). Woodbine House Publishers.
An excellent collection of more than one thousand books and other resources about disabilities for parents of children with special needs. In addition to extensive subject and title indexes, this book also includes listings of organizations, parent advocacy groups, and professional agencies.

Beer, W. R. (1992). *American stepfamilies.* New Brunswick, NJ: Transaction Publishers.
The author presents an overview of special concerns that face stepfamilies, particularly adult relationships and parent–child interactions. Extensive use of case histories and personal experiences lends a unique and sensitive insight into an often misunderstood family patterns.

Brooks, J. B. (1996). *Parenting.* Mountain View, CA: Mayfield Publishing Company.
A comprehensive book that addresses many contemporary parenting issues. Information on behavior management and developmentally appropriate expectations are included for children at all stages along the developmental continuum. Special attention is also given to issues of working parents, the single parent, stepparenting, and children with specific needs.

Christopherson, E. R. (1990). *Beyond discipline: Parenting that lasts a lifetime.* Kansas City, KS: Westport Publishers.
This respected authority on child development and behavior management tackles a universal concern of parents and teachers with his usual wit and humor. His techniques have evolved from extensive research and years of clinical experience with young children.

Eisenberg, A., Murkoff, H., and Hathway, S. (1996). *What to expect: The first year.* NY: Workman Publishers.

Eisenberg, A., Murkoff, H., and Hathway, S. (1996). *What to expect: The toddler years.* NY: Workman Publishers.

Both of these books provide a wealth of down-to-earth information about very young children for new, as well as experienced, parents and caregivers. Excellent coverage of child development and caregiving routines is provided in an easy to understand manner. These just may be the baby owner's manuals that every parent searches for.

Hamner, T., and Turner, P. (1996). *Parenting in contemporary society.* Needham Heights, MA: Allyn & Bacon.
Examines the diversity of traditional and nontraditional family patterns in the United States, along with cultural differences, socioeconomic variations, working families, high-risk families, and adoption and foster care, as well as families of exceptional children. Throughout this book, emphasis is placed on effective parenting strategies.

Jaffe, M. L. (1996). *Understanding parenting.* New York: Wm. C. Brown Publishers.
A review focus is on child-rearing problems that typically confront parents and caregivers of young children through adolescents. The importance of good parent–child relationships and communication is stressed throughout the text.

Marotz, L., Cross, M., and Rush, J. (1997). *Health, safety, and nutrition for the young child* (4th ed.). Albany, NY: Delmar Publishers.
A comprehensive overview of the numerous factors that enhance children's growth and development. It includes some of the most current research information and knowledge concerning each of these areas, and is especially useful for parents and caregivers.

Parenting: An ecological perspective. (1993). T. Luster and L. Okagaki (Eds.). Hillsdale, NJ: Lawrence Erlbaum Associates, Publishers.
An up-to-date compilation of research findings on a variety of contemporary issues related to differences in parenting behavior. These multidisciplinary studies were undertaken in an effort to improve the understanding of parental behavior and how to effectively enhance parent–child relationships.

Watson, L., Watson, M., and Wilson, L. C. (1999). *Infants and toddlers* (4th ed.). Albany, NY: Delmar Publishers.
Parents and caregivers will find this book particularly useful in understanding developmental sequences, creating enriching environments, and providing appropriate learning experiences for infants and toddlers based on their developmental needs.

Weiser, M. (1991). *Infant/toddler care and education.* New York: Macmillan Publishing Company.
Another comprehensive book that focuses on the major aspects of care and educational approaches unique to the infant and toddler. This book is designed for parents and caregivers of children under three years of age.

INDEX